# Henry B. Gonzalez

## *Rebel with a Cause*

## Jean Flynn

EAKIN PRESS ⴎ Austin, Texas

FIRST EDITION
Copyright © 2004
By Jean Flynn
Published in the United States of America
By Eakin Press
A Division of Sunbelt Media, Inc.
P.O. Drawer 90159 ☜ Austin, Texas 78709-0159
email: sales@eakinpress.com
💻 website: www.eakinpress.com 💻
1  2  3  4  5  6  7  8  9
**1-57168-780-7 HB**
**1-57168-846-3 PB**

**Library of Congress Cataloging-in-Publication Data**

Flynn, Jean
    Henry B. Gonzalez : rebel with a cause / by Jean Flynn.–1st ed.
        p.  cm.
    Summary: A biography of the first Mexican American elected to the
United States Congress from Texas, the times in which he lived, and some
of the problems he confronted.
    Includes biographical references and index.
    ISBN 1-57168-780-7
    1. Gonzalez, Henry B. (Henry Barbosa), 1916–Juvenile literature.
2. Legislators–United States. Congress. House–Biography–Juvenile literature. 4. Mexican Legislators–Texas–Biography–Juvenile literature. 5.
Legislators–Texas–Biography–Juvenile literature. 6. Texas. Legislature.
Senate–Biography–Juvenile literature. 7. Texas–Politics and government–1951–Juvenile literature. [1. Gonzalez, Henry B. (Henry Barbosa),
1916- 2. Legislators. 3. Mexian Americans–Biography. 4. Texas–Politics
and government.] I. Title
E840.8.G63F58    2002
328.73'092–dc21                                                    2002156753

*For Kitty and Paul Baker*

# CONTENTS

# CHAPTER 1

# *El Don de la Gente*

*"El don de la gente,"* "maverick," "Meskin greaser," "fighter," "fearless trailblazer," "hot-headed Meskin," "witty," "quixotic," "vengeful," "loyal," "eccentric," "irascible," "dirty dog," "passionate," "populist," "ultimate outsider," "a loner," "a white taco." These were among the many ways Enrique Barbosa Gonzalez was described. But he was called "Henry B." by all who knew him, friends and enemies. Anything written or said about Henry B., whether affectionate or critical, described him in a vivid way, because he was so colorful in speech and in dress. He was loved by the press for his quick-witted one-liners. He was disliked by his enemies because of his quick responses.

"You either loved or hated Henry. Nobody felt indifferent toward him," said Bertha Gonzalez, his wife of sixty years.[1] Henry B.'s friends respected and loved him. His enemies respected and feared him. Some hated him because he was *el don de la gente*—a man of the people. He took care of the people he represented without regard to power, politics, or money. He helped whoever asked, regardless of political party, race, or income level.

1

## Time of War

Many things influenced Henry B.'s philosophy of life and his politics. Those same influences created in him a one-of-a-kind maverick. In 1916, the year of Henry B.'s birth, "Uncle Sam" was born in the United States. A portrait of Uncle Sam with the slogan "What are you doing for preparedness?" appeared on the cover of *Leslie's Weekly*. The image went on to become the most popular military recruiting poster of all time. Henry B. grew up with that image. And no one could have done more to prepare for a life of service.

Henry B. was born into a world of war. Animosity between the United States and Mexico was growing intense. Mexican bandit Francisco "Pancho" Villa and his band of rebels ordered sixteen American mining engineers to exit a train near Chihuahua City, then shot them. The United States was on the brink of joining World War I.

Henry B.'s parents had lived through the Mexican Revolution, escaping from Mexico with their lives and little else. His father, Leonides Gonzalez, had been a wealthy landowner, mayor, and mine owner in Mapini, Mexico. He had escaped death by a firing squad at the hands of revolutionaries in the 1911 uprising against the tyranny of Porfirio Díaz.

## Immigrants from Mexico

When the once-wealthy family arrived in San Antonio, all of the Gonzalez fortune had been left behind. Leonides Gonzalez was one of many Mexican immigrants who did not speak English. He supported his wife and two sons by doing odd jobs and selling advertisements for Spanish-language newspapers. By the time Henry B. was born in 1916, Gonzalez was general manager of *La Prensa,* a Spanish-language daily newspaper. *La Prensa* was the voice of Mexican politicians and intellectuals who had settled in San Antonio. The Gonzalez home became a gathering place for refugees. Henry B. often awoke to hear historians, orators, generals, and journalists talking through the night.

Those intellectuals influenced Henry B. throughout his life. He loved the sounds and rhythms of language. As a child he spent his spare time at the public library. He read the books in his father's library and those his father brought home from *La Prensa.* He read history, biography, law, and philosophy. He often copied, word for word, passages that he particularly liked. He later drew from those passages in making speeches before the Texas Senate and the U.S. House of Representatives.

## A World of Prejudice

Another influence on Henry B.'s life was prejudice. He was not allowed to sit down in restaurants where Anglos ate. He could not drink from certain water fountains. He and his friends were allowed to use only one city park, because of segregation. Public schools were segregated by race. People made fun of his accent, so he worked daily to improve his speech. He also studied and read languages other than Spanish and English.[2]

Of all the things Henry B. was called, perhaps "passionate" would best describe him. He was passionate about desegregating Texas and the United States. As a city councilman, he led the fight to integrate San Antonio's public swimming pools. By running for governor against Price

Daniel, a segregationist, he brought the issue of race before voters. He holds the record for the longest filibuster in the Texas House of Representatives, to defeat fourteen race bills designed to keep public schools segregated.

## An American First

In 1961, Henry B. became the first American of Mexican descent to win a seat in the U.S. House of Representatives. New or freshman members were expected to be quiet—seen but not heard. But Henry B. spoke out loudly against the poll tax. Throughout the South, the poll tax had kept poor African Americans from voting. In Texas, Henry B. had seen how the tax affected poor Mexican Americans, as well. Others in Congress got the message. Henry B. was not going to be quiet. And he would not be ignored.

As the congressman from Texas, he was the champion of civil rights, affordable housing, and safe banking practices for all Americans. Often a lone voice in Congress, Henry B. warned fellow legislators of an impending savings-and-loan crisis. His critics laughed at him and called him quixotic, but the warnings proved prophetic. He sponsored and passed laws that reformed the savings-and-loan industry and established interstate banking. Thousands of senior citizens and poor people would have lost their life savings without his leadership in passing laws.

He set the example for other Mexican Americans who wanted to enter politics. He was every young Mexican American politician's dream. They all wanted to be like Henry B. His influence reached from the West Side *barrios* of San Antonio, across Texas, and then throughout the nation. He was a fearless trailblazer in his fight for minorities and the poor. He proved that a Mexican American could succeed in an Anglo world. He inspired many Mexican American students. He was a role model in the civil rights movement. He spoke for people who had no voice in local, state, or national government.

Henry B. was often referred to as the ultimate outsider, but no one could criticize him for his honesty. When he ran for Congress in 1961, he turned his back on money from special-interest groups. His opponent campaigned in the West Side of San Antonio by furnishing food and drink to the voters. When Henry B. campaigned without money, he told the voters, "You can drink his beer and eat his tamales. But when you go to the polls, vote for Gonzalez."[3]

When Henry B. went to Congress in 1961, he took his populist beliefs with him—he believed in the rights of the common people. He supported President John F. Kennedy's civil rights initiatives and later approved of President Lyndon B. Johnson's Great Society programs. President Johnson once remarked, "I don't have to worry about Henry. Henry's for the people."[4] Henry B. was responsible for getting millions of dollars in federal grants for housing, hospitals, schools, and military bases in the San Antonio area.

## Fighting Windmills

Henry B.'s critics said he was always "fighting windmills," comparing him to the literary character Don Quixote, who thought windmills were enemy giants. But as one critic grudgingly said of him, "As soon as everybody is about to write him off, he comes up with something that history proves him right about."[5] Henry B. cared more about his moral responsibilities than about power. He sometimes refused the president's phone calls. One upset president was overheard saying, "Henry, you understand I *am* the president!"[6]

He never refused a constituent's request, though. He was the ideal example of a public servant, working solely for the benefit of his 20th Congressional District. For days after his death, the *San Antonio Express-News* was filled with letters from people he had helped. No issue, no person was too small for his attention. The signs outside his office doors in both Washington and San Antonio read: "This office belongs to the people of the 20th District of Texas." He never forgot who sent him to Washington. He never forgot where he came from or who he was.

Who was this "ultimate outsider" who won political offices again and again? This relentless "political burr" who believed in the rights, wisdom, and virtues of the common people?

---

"What I care about is what you care about—decency, justice, an abhorrence for what is wrong, and an intolerance for mediocrity."

—Henry B. Gonzalez

# CHAPTER 2

# *The Maverick*

"Being a maverick is a badge of honor to me," Henry B. often told journalists.[1] He came from a long line of mavericks. His forefathers, who would not accept tyranny from the Mexican government, fought for separation of church and state. His great-great-grandfather, Joaquin Lugo Cigarroa, was a leader of the liberal forces who resisted General Santa Anna. His Spanish ancestors settled in the state of Durango in northern Mexico in 1561, fifteen years after silver was discovered there. They became wealthy ranchers and silver-mine owners. So great was their wealth that when Henry B.'s great-grandmother married, "her father [Joaquin] ordered a pathway paved of silver from the door of the house to the door of the church."[2] For eight generations, Gonzalez's forefathers were mayors of Mapimi, a silver mining center west of Monterrey, Mexico.

## The Beginning of the Mexican Revolution

Henry B.'s grandfather, also named Joaquin, was friends with Benito Juárez, one of Mexico's great heroes. Juárez, a

7

poor Indian, became a lawyer, judge, governor, and finally the president of Mexico. He fought the clergy, who ruled with unreasonable and severe laws. He established a democratic federal republic that took the power from the clergy and church and gave it to the government. Henry B.'s grandfather Joaquin worked with Juárez in the struggle for the separation of church and state. After Juárez's death, another poor Indian, Porfirio Díaz, became president. Leonides Gonzalez, Henry B.'s father, worked for President Porfirio Díaz until the Mexican Revolution began in 1910.

On Henry B.'s mother's side of the family, his great-great-grandfather was a Scotch-Irish Presbyterian from Londonderry. He arrived in northern Mexico from Pennsylvania in the 1850s and built the first textile mill in the area. His maternal grandmother was named McMunn Bornhof Prince. Henry B. was proud of his Irish ancestors. He once teased President John F. Kennedy, "We Irish have to stick together."[3]

## Rule by the Wealthy

Porfirio Díaz was a general, and he ruled like a dictator. His policies created wealth, but it was in the hands of a few while the masses remained very poor. Land was taken from more than a million families. They had nowhere to go. There was an oversupply of laborers for the jobs available. It was cheaper to hire a man than it was to rent a mule. The people's lives were miserable: they lived in dirty, overcrowded huts, lacked proper food, and suffered from disability, disease, and death.[4]

President Díaz appointed all important federal, state, and local officials, including the *jefe politico,* a local official who watched all the other officials in his district and reported directly to Díaz. Henry B.'s father, Leonides Gonzalez, mayor of the mining town of Mapimi, was appointed *jefe político.*

Leonides and Genoveva Gonzalez, Henry B.'s parents, had two sons, Leonides and Carlos, by the time the Mexican Revolution began. They lived in a mansion on the town square and had many servants as well as many mine workers. Their home was attached to the Cigarroa home. The two homes formed an "L" that went around two sides of a deep block on the corner of the plaza. The two houses shared a common patio and were connected on the second floor. Houses, patios, and smaller buildings took up the whole block. Leonides owned and operated silver mines in the Mapimi basin. Silver from the mines was taken by ox cart over the Sierra Mountains and was sold to Chinese merchants.

Wealthy families hid silver and jewelry to keep the government and bandits from taking it. Compartments were dug into the thick adobe walls, which were sometimes six feet thick. Although Leonides Gonzalez did not confirm it, the family told a story about him finding money in an adobe wall. The story was that in 1902, while rebuilding an adobe stable, he discovered a half-million dollars in silver hidden in the wall.[5] But when he left Mexico, he lost all of his wealth.

## The Mexican Revolution

In 1909, Francisco Madero wrote tracts against Díaz's reelection and for democracy. Madero was a rich and well-educated man. When Díaz again declared himself reelected, Madero was jailed. He was able to escape and went to San Antonio, and from there he proclaimed a day of uprising in Mexico. In Chihuahua, Pancho Villa organized the poor and the landless against the *haciendas* and mine owners. In Morelos, Zapata organized the Army of the South. They began killing landlords and burning the *haciendas*.

Leonides Gonzalez decided to stay in his home and continue his business. In early 1911, different groups, some revolutionists and some bandits, began roaming the countryside and taking over towns. A large group entered Mapimi and captured it. A small band of drunks took Leonides Gonzalez to execute him because he was a wealthy man and one of Diaz's officials, but Juana Lopez, a merchant's wife, rescued him. Prior to the outbreak of the revolution, there had been a group of bandits in the mountains who raided towns and homes and then went back to their hideaway. Juana Lopez's husband and son had been arrested and accused of being bandits. Charged with treason, they were sentenced to be executed. Leonides Gonzalez knew that the two were innocent. The local colonels and political officials bitterly disagreed, but Leonides freed the two men. Juana Lopez remembered his help and brought her own band of men to free him. Leonides agreed to give over all of his possessions and leave the country in exchange for his life. She ordered the band to turn him loose. When they released him, she chased the bandits off. She gave Leonides a horse, and he rode with the group to a railroad trestle. She pointed to a group of riflemen on the trestle who were to have been Leonides' executioners.[6]

## Escape to San Antonio

Leonides sent word to his wife to go to Monterrey. Genoveva took their two sons, Leonides and Carlos, her aunt, and their nanny, Angelita, and left in the middle of the night. She took what money and jewels she could hide in her clothes. Leonides met his wife in Monterrey, and they took the train north to Laredo. They didn't like Laredo and went on to San Antonio, arriving on February 8, 1911. The family "looked like *Hungaros*" (gypsies) when they arrived carrying all of their possessions.[7] For several weeks they lived in the Gunther Hotel, until they had used all of the money Genoveva had smuggled from Mexico.

Leonides didn't speak English. The former aristocrat had to take what jobs he could get. He worked at a drug store, then a grocery store. He sold ads for Spanish-language newspapers and did odd jobs to support his family. He advanced from selling advertisements for *La Prensa* to become managing editor in 1913, and he eventually retired as publisher. When he had a stable salary, the family bought a house at 217 Upson Street, near downtown San Antonio.

## Displaced Mexican Citizens

Due to Leonides' work at *La Prensa,* the Gonzalez house was the meeting place for Mexican refugees who had moved to San Antonio. The refugees, including Leonides, believed they would someday return to Mexico, where they would regain their wealth. It was in that environment of displaced Mexican citizens that Henry B. was born on May 3, 1916.

The refugees had fled Mexico to preserve their values, including love of family and respect for their country. All conversations centered around what was happening in Mexico. Leonides and Genoveva encouraged their children to get a good education before they returned "home." The opportunity for a good education was unlikely in Mexico.

The talk of his parents and their friends about returning "home" confused Henry B. as a child. He knew he had

11

been born in San Antonio, which was in the United States of America. But his parents never referred to San Antonio or America as "home."

The children studied American history and spoke and wrote in English. Their friends were immigrant children, but they knew nothing about Mexico except what they heard in their households. All of the immigrant children were confused about their nationality.

## Head of the Household

The Gonzalez family was tightly knit. Leonides was the unchallenged head of the household. He ruled with a stern hand and demanded complete obedience from his five sons and one daughter. The family was very regimented about eating dinner together. The meal was considered discussion time. The children told about their day, and the family discussed ideas learned from their studies. Their father told them about Mexico. Nana, their housekeeper and governess, had come from Mexico with them and was part of the household. When Henry B. said, "I am an American," she was angry. She told him, *"Acaso un gato nace en un horno es pan"*— "I guess if a cat's born in an oven it makes him bread."[8]

"He had one foot in the United States and one foot in Mexico," said his son Charlie.[9] Henry B. didn't know if he was Mexican or American.

---

Henry B. was openly opposed to such hyphenated terms as *Latin-American* and liked to quote Maury Maverick's statement that "a Latin-American is a Mexican with a poll tax receipt."[10]

12

# CHAPTER 3

# *Meskin Greaser*

"Meskin greaser" was a term young Henry B. heard often. He was born into a world of intellectuals, but he was treated by outsiders as if he were stupid. He was also born into a world of segregation and prejudice. The neighborhood in which the Gonzalez family lived was considered middle-class. There were Anglos, German Americans, and Mexican Americans. There was a mixture of well-off people and the poor, the educated and the rough uneducated. Schools were segregated by race. Many minority children had to walk past the Anglo elementary school to get to their own school. Minorities were barred from restaurants, cafes, and recreational areas. If they were allowed inside a cafe for a cold drink, they had to stand up to drink it. African Americans had to go to the back door of a restaurant or cafe to get service and stand in the alley while the order was prepared.

Henry B.'s parents did not speak English. Spanish was his first language, and he could not speak English when he began first grade. Because of the language barrier, he stayed in low first grade for a full year. Children were not allowed to speak Spanish at school. The majority of the teachers spoke only English. For the most part, though, Henry B. had good teachers who understood the children's problems. He often told his own children about all the wonderful teachers he had in school. He remembered how they had worked with him to help him reach his potential. Each child was a challenge, including Henry B.[1] There was one bad experience that he never forgot, however:

"What do you mean, you little Comanche? I'm going to wash your mouth. Little Mexican!" his second-grade teacher said to him when she heard him speak Spanish.[2] He was so upset that he knocked a glass of water out of her hand and ran home. His parents believed that education was the way to get ahead in life. They encouraged their children to do well in school. His mother took him back to Stephen F. Austin Elementary School to finish the day. The experience stayed in his memory for his lifetime, but it did not keep him from being an avid reader and quick learner. Once he learned English, he advanced quickly and skipped a grade in school.

## Mexican or American?

Leonides Gonzalez unintentionally confused Henry B. about his nationality. Because he had never intended to stay in the United States, he regarded himself and his family as Mexican citizens, even the children born in San Antonio. He planned to take his family back to Mexico as soon as the Mexican Revolution ended. Henry did not know whether he was Mexican or American. Miss Mason, his third-grade teacher, cleared up his confusion when she was preparing his permanent school record.

"Are you a U.S. citizen?" she asked Henry B.

"I'm a Mexican," he replied.

"Where were you born?" she asked.

"San Antonio," said Henry B.

"You're an American," she told him.[3]

He didn't know whether to believe it or not. Henry B. later said he was twenty years old before he fully overcame his uncertainties about his nationality. Even though his family roots were in Mexico, he frequently said, "But I am an American and my first and last loyalty is to America—the United States of America."[4]

## A New Discovery

Henry B. discovered the world of books in the public library when he was eight years old. He could not speak English well, but he could read it. He spent as much time as he could in the library. He first read westerns. As he gained more confidence, his choices became history, biographies, law, and philosophy. He copied entire essays by Matthew Arnold because he liked the sound of the words. By the time he was sixteen, he had read all the old masters: Ortega y Gasset's *Revolt of the Masses,* Thiers' history of the French Revolution, Thomas Carlyle, and others.

He had a special relationship with his father. He read books written in Spanish that his father brought home from *La Prensa.* He was the only one of the children who liked to read in Spanish. The father and son discussed books both had read. "There seemed to be more communication between Papa and Henry than between Papa and the rest of us," Joaquin, Henry B.'s brother, said.[5]

## Problems with English

Henry B. had no problem reading. He had problems speaking English. His accent was so heavy that even his friends made fun of him. He had read that Demosthenes of Athens developed his speaking skills by shouting at the sea with pebbles in his mouth. At night he read aloud with marbles in his mouth, speaking into a fan to create an ocean breeze, "until Papa thought I was nuts and told me to stop," he said.[6] He read aloud from Robert Louis Stevenson and had a friend correct his pronunciation. At night he spoke to himself in a mirror. His four brothers and a sister slipped outside and watched him through a window. When they couldn't keep from laughing at him, they ran away. But it worked for him. He eventually spoke flawless English.[7]

## After-School Jobs

Henry B. was ten years old when he went to work for Ernst von Helms, a retired German sea captain. It was his first after-school job. Von Helms, who owned a drug store, was a strict boss who frightened away delivery boys. He gave orders half in German and half in broken English. "Enrico," as von Helms called him, was not so easily frightened. He worked for von Helms for more than a year, becoming part-time clerk and soda jerk. Von Helms taught him to mop, to speak a little German, and to be self-reliant and resourceful.

Von Helms was interested in world politics and had long discussions with his customers. When he could not recall a date or name or fact, he turned to Henry B. for the answer. "Enrico knows," he said.[8] Von Helms was a patriotic German. Henry B. assumed that everyone was filled with love and devotion of one's native country.

Henry B. sold Crowell magazines like *Woman's Home Companion, Collier's,* and *American* after he left von Helms' employment. He had a paper route for the *San Antonio Light* until he figured out his profit. He had made only $1.60 in three months. He worked for a while at a Red and White grocery store run by Chinese people. He had no problems getting a job, because he was a quick learner and hard worker.

## Growing up on the West Side

The Riverside gang was the bully group in the West Side neighborhood where Henry B. grew up. They picked on boys who were not in the gang. Henry B. organized a group himself. The worst thing they did was raid a neighborhood grocer's cookie barrel. One of the boys distracted the merchant while the others sneaked in and grabbed handfuls of cookies. They quit when two boys were caught making their own raid. Henry B. was never caught, although he was a prime suspect. Some of the Riverside gang members eventually got into serious trouble and went to prison.

Years later, Henry B. would say in speeches that his life was an open book, except for a couple of periods during his adolescence. Actually, he created few discipline problems for his parents because he didn't have time to get into trouble. Once, during a rough-and-tumble exchange in the Texas Senate, he said, "I had to come up through the jungle of the West Side and I think I know how it is to have to fight alley-fashion."[9]

The West Side influenced Henry B. all of his life. He never forgot his best friend's mother, who went blind. She handsewed baby garments for a nickel apiece. She worked in her home from five in the morning until eleven at night. Many neighborhood women handsewed for the same factory. They gathered each day and took their garments to the factory for their pay. They averaged about $1 a day each. "If there was something wrong with some of the stitches," Henry B. said later, "they would ask them to unstitch them right in front of them, and tell them that you don't get paid for that."[10]

## A Lone Wolf

Henry B. was athletic and enjoyed playing sandlot football, baseball, and basketball. He boxed in gymnastics and sparred with his cousins and friends in the back yard. They encouraged him to fight. If he didn't win the first time, he fought again until he defeated his opponent. He excelled in events that required individual effort. From early in life, Henry B. was somewhat of a "lone wolf."[11] He attended Mark Twain Junior High School, where he was a good student.[12] He went to Main Avenue High School until Jefferson High opened. After he graduated from Jefferson in 1935, he attended San Antonio Junior College. He specialized in pre-engineering courses and earned an associate's degree in 1937. His professors recognized his abilities and encouraged him to continue his education.

Henry B. enrolled at the University of Texas at Austin, where his brother Joaquin was studying. They shared a room in a boarding house run by two spinster sisters. The young men cleaned rooms for one meal a day. Henry B. also worked twenty hours a week for five dollars with the Austin Exterminating Company. He found odd jobs to add to his income. He was a translator in a district court insurance case. He impressed the judge so much that his pay was doubled.[13]

Henry B. was also an amateur boxer during that time. He competed in both San Antonio and Austin. He often joked that "boxing gave me this nose."[14] "Dad boxed at the San Fernando gym as a sport where he once got a money prize. Ultimately he was opposed to professional boxing," said his son, Henry B. Jr. "He witnessed a semi-professional fight one time and saw the violence and brutality and money involved. It changed his whole opinion about boxing."[15] Later, as a legislator, Henry B. was criticized for introducing legislation to ban boxing. "What legislators do as young people may not be what they do as adults," said Henry B. Jr. "They aren't given credit for maturing and seeing things in a different light."[16]

## A Hard Winter in Austin

Joaquin and Henry B. spent a cold and hungry winter in Austin. They could not afford a heater and used newspapers as blankets. Their one meal a day was not enough, and they were often hungry. Austin was not an easy town for Mexican Americans. Students of Mexican descent could not get jobs near the campus and had to go across town to work. They were not free to choose a cafe of their choice, even if they had had money to go there. They were often called "greasers" or "spics."[17] Although they had experienced the same prejudice in San Antonio, they had their family and friends for some security. In Austin they had no one.

Joaquin was able to join the Texas part of the National

Youth Administration, which was overseen by Lyndon B. Johnson. Only one person from a family could be a member of the workforce. When Henry B. lost his jobs and developed anemia, he decided to return home. The Great Depression was on, and jobs were difficult to find. His family needed him to help out as well as pay his own tuition. As soon as he was able, he enrolled in St. Mary's University School of Law.

## A Talented Family

Leonides and Genoveva Gonzalez couldn't afford college tuition for their children, but they expected them to go to college. They did not speak English, but they trained their children in manners and cultural things and to have inquisitive minds. They taught them to have pride in themselves. There was a high standard of expectation that each of the children met. While most of the family played the piano, Luz, the only daughter, was the talented musician. Carlos was good at math and lectured classes while he was still working on a degree from Rice University. Melchor was a natural athlete and excelled in football at Jefferson High School. He thought he would get a scholarship to attend A&M, but "Mexicans" were not awarded scholarships.[18] Joaquin became a medical doctor. Leonides Jr., the oldest, became a mining engineer and eventually returned to Mexico.

But Henry B. had a distraction from studies and work. Bertha Cuellar had come into his life.

"It was a time when things were so tough that if a dog bit a Mexican, they'd kill the Mexican, send his head to Austin for analysis, and give the dog rabies shots."

—Henry B. Gonzalez

---

"My citizenship is not in any way qualified. I am an American, plain and simple, and as it happens, I am of Mexican descent."

—Henry B. Gonzalez

# CHAPTER 4

# *Dirty Dog*

"That dirty dog was telling everyone that we were going steady, and we weren't even going around together," Bertha laughed, eyes sparkling.[1] But Henry B. met his match in 1938: petite, pretty, and lively Bertha Cuellar.

Bertha was born on November 21, 1917, in Floresville, Texas. Her parents were Lino Eduardo and Francesca (Frances) Cuellar. Her mother was half Mexican and half German. Her father was five years old when his family emigrated from Spain. Bertha's family can be traced back to some of the original Spanish colonizers in Texas. Her grandfather was a U.S. marshall in the Rio Grande Valley. Her father worked as a linotypist at Sam Fore's *Chronicle* in Floresville. Bertha was one of seven children, one boy and six girls. It was through her sister Oralia that she met Henry B.

Luz, Henry B.'s sister, and Oralia were doing post-graduate study at Texas Tech. During the summer, Luz visited Oralia in Floresville, where the Cuellar family lived. Henry drove her there because women were discouraged from driving alone. Bertha thought he was "a little full of himself." He thought she was "a snappy little thing" and called her a "tiger." Bertha preferred to be called "Chihuahua," which became a joke between them over the years.[2] While Luz and Oralia talked about "girl things," Bertha and Henry B. talked about books. They were both "book-worms." She was glad to have someone to talk to about something besides sports or boys. And he was glad to talk to someone who liked to read.[3]

## Henry B. Courts Bertha

"Backward" was what Henry B. called himself when it came to girls. He was twenty-two before he had a date. "I was 'backward' socially," he once said.[4] "He was a comedian at heart but he was never sociable," Bertha said.[5] Bertha saw through his comedy routines, which were a cover for shyness. But he "learned with Bertha," he often teased.[6] When Bertha was in high school, her family moved to San Antonio. Her mother and Henry B.'s mother became good friends and belonged to the same bridge club. Henry B. drove his mother, and Bertha tagged along with her mother because Bertha did not drive.

He often brought his mother to the Cuellar house to visit. Bertha and Henry B. sat on the porch and talked while their mothers visited inside. They were not "romanti-cally involved," although Henry B. seemed "to hang around the house a lot," Bertha remembered with a chuckle.[7] One day he sat down in the same chair as Bertha. Luz said, "Henry, why don't you move to another chair?"

He said, "Why? I'm doing just fine here," and put his arm around her. The little "tiger" did not object to sharing her chair.[8]

Social dances were chaperoned by mothers of the young women. The mothers went with their daughters to all dances, whether at the Casino Club or the neighborhood club. The young people called the mothers "the Gestapo." The women sat around on the outside of the dance floor, watching the young people. If a girl danced three dances in a row with the same young man, her mother gave her "the eye," which meant disapproval. Henry B. danced like he did everything else—full speed ahead! He was much taller than Bertha, and she often had to tell him to slow down. Henry B. didn't like to dance as much as Bertha did. They often ended up talking about books at one end of the dance floor. Bertha was a good dancer and had never lacked for partners. Then she realized that no one but Henry B. was asking her to dance anymore. That was when she found out that "the dirty dog" had told everyone they were going steady. "After that, things got serious," she laughed.[9]

Henry B. was a year older than Bertha. He was in his first year at the University of Texas. She was a senior at Brackenridge High School. Both sets of parents thought they were getting too serious. "And if they had known how serious, they had a right to be worried," Bertha said, her eyes twinkling at the memory.[10] Her parents made a rule that the young couple could see each other only one day on the weekend. When Henry B. came home for the summer, his parents sent him to his brother's ranch in Monclovo, Mexico.

## Rebel with a Cause

Henry B. thought he was going to Mexico for a week's visit. Once he got there, his family took away his money.

24

His brother and parents had planned to keep him there all summer. Bertha and Henry B. wrote letters every day. Bertha cried every time she received a letter. "My sister used to cry with me," she said. "Henry was a rebel with a cause. They couldn't keep him there." Henry B. "borrowed" a horse from his brother and rode to the train station. He tied the horse where it would be found and jumped on the train as a hobo. He showed up at Bertha's house "all dirty and ragged." She barely recognized him. "They are not going to keep me there," Henry B. declared.[11]

His parents were angry with him. Her parents were worried about her. But nothing could keep Henry B. and Bertha apart.

Bertha developed tuberculosis and could not finish high school. At that time, anyone with tuberculosis was isolated, because it was believed to be contagious. She was homebound for a year. That did not discourage Henry B. He sat in the room next to hers and sang to her. By then he was enrolled in St. Mary's University School of Law and visited her every day. When she recovered from her illness, she returned to Brackenridge High School and graduated. Their parents finally consented to their marriage. Henry B. and Bertha were married in the St. Philip Catholic church on November 10, 1940.

## Graduation without a Diploma

Tuition for law school was expensive and had to be earned, because Henry B.'s parents could not afford to pay it for him. It was difficult for a young married man to support himself and a wife and pay tuition. They lived with one of Bertha's sisters, and Henry B. worked in the law library for $30 a month. He got a part-time job with the city as a clerk in the Ehrenborg Tax Resurvey. He served in naval intelligence after war was declared on Japan on December 8, 1941. But when it came time to graduate in 1943, he did not receive his diploma. He walked across the stage at graduation, but he was given a blank paper. It was several months later that he paid off his debt. He had earned the money by working for Louie's Cut-Rate Drugs for $12 weekly and at a package store as manager for $14 weekly. He finally received his diploma.[12]

Henry B. graduated from St. Mary's University Law School, but he never completed the bar exam. He went to Austin to take the exam and was forced to leave in the middle of the test because of a boil that closed his left eye. Although he prepared for the bar at later times, he never again took the bar examination and never practiced law. He did eventually have three lawyer sons: Henry B. Jr., Charlie, and Frank. "He was always interested in what Charlie, Frank, and I were doing and talked to us about the changes in law," said Henry B. Jr.[13]

## The Family Grows

Henry B. and Bertha's first child, Henry B. Jr., was born prematurely in 1941. He weighed only three pounds. Bertha and Henry didn't know how to take care of a baby, much less one so small. They moved into his parents' house so Mrs. Gonzalez could help Bertha with the baby. It was an around-the-clock job with little sleep.

Henry B. Jr. had to be fed every thirty minutes with a large eyedropper. He was so small that regular diapers wouldn't fit. Mr. Gonzalez came home one day with two dozen men's handkerchiefs for diapers. The diapers had to be rinsed, boiled, rinsed again, hung out to dry, and then ironed every day. Even with all the work, Henry Jr. developed a terrible rash. Mrs. Gonzalez helped Bertha with the feedings and diapers so she could get some rest.

Henry B. Jr. didn't walk until he was almost two years old. He scooted all over the place and had to be watched all the time. They had a German shepherd dog that watched over him and brought him back by the diaper if he went too far. Long before Henry B. Jr. learned to walk, he was joined by a sister, Rose Mary, in August 1942.

## San Antonio Changes

While Henry B. was concentrating on his education and supporting a growing family, the city of San Antonio was rapidly changing. During the first thirty years of the twentieth century, San Antonio quadrupled its size to almost a quarter of a million people. The Mexican American population jumped from 23 percent to 35 percent. They were relatively segregated on the west side of town. Many were living in disease, poverty, filth, and illiteracy. A nationally noted correspondent called San Antonio's slums "the worst in America."[14]

The Anglo community's only contact with Mexican Americans was when they did its labor. The community was indifferent to the Mexican Americans' presence. Few were aware of the part of the city that was full of disease, poverty, illiteracy, and filth. The Great Depression added to the problem. There were not enough jobs to go around. When there was a choice between an Anglo or Mexican American, the Anglo got the job. When the city's civic leaders realized that the Mexican American population was increasing by a twenty-to-one ratio, they appointed an official fact-finding committee to study the issue.

The committee, made up of civic leaders, concluded that in San Antonio and its suburbs, the Mexican American population was the most serious problem. When the problem was pinpointed, the next step was to remove it. The committee recommended: "It is believed that consideration should be given to the redistribution of population, and that some of these families should voluntarily return to the small towns and farms from which they have come and that other families should be returned to Mexico."[15]

The Mexican American problem was a serious one. Fifty-three percent of the population lived in substandard housing. Lack of indoor plumbing led to fly breeding, communicable diseases, and child intestinal disorders. Diarrhea and tuberculosis were the number-one killers. Infant death rate was twice the national average. A child who survived had little chance of an education. Only one-half completed first grade, a fourth eighth grade, a tenth high school, and one out of 200 went to college.[16]

## World War II Declared

World War II took the attention from San Antonio's problems as the world focused on Adolph Hitler. When Pearl Harbor was attacked on December 7, 1942, Henry B. was called into military intelligence as a translator, interpreter, and censor. He worked in San Antonio on mail, radio, phone, and telegraph communications. He could speak not only Spanish and English, but also German. (He later learned Portuguese and Italian.) German U-boats were able to get in between the Texas coast and merchant ships and then torpedo them. There were people in Mexico who would lose money if Germany lost the war. They were helping Nazi agents coordinate the attacks on the merchant ships. Henry B. overheard a conversation and was able to figure out that Nazi agents in Tampico were giving their submarines the sailing dates of all the ships up and down the Gulf Coast. "We not only broke up that little nest," he said, "I think I saved the United States about $1 million on stockpiling materials in Mexico."[17]

In 1944 Henry B. was offered a commission as ensign in the Navy. The commission would have assured him veterans' benefits after the war. He didn't accept it, because he didn't want to leave his growing family. He decided to apply for a position with the FBI. He passed the tests but was not accepted. "No opening," he was told, but he believed it was because he was Mexican American. "Oh, they were very racist," he said.[18] He instead became assistant juvenile probation officer of Bexar County. He was happy to get the job, because his family was still growing. His son Charles (Charlie) was born in May 1945.

## Education for All Veterans

There was economic improvement in San Antonio because of the military bases after World War II. Mexican American men had fought in the war and had veterans' benefits but were still segregated. One of their veterans' rights was the GI Bill, which paid for education. Many took advantage of it and finished high school and college. As they became more educated, they became more politically aware.

They protested the segregation of their children in public schools. They felt they were illegally classified as a separate race. They protested the restriction in contracts that kept them from buying property outside the slums. By 1948, West Side Mexican Americans joined forces with the African Americans on the East Side community to elect Mexican American attorney Gus Garcia and African American G. J. Sutton as a junior college trustee. The anonymous writer "Don Politico" predicted in the *San Antonio Light* that "now citizens' groups, even from the West Side, will be heard."[19] Although it was a major breakthrough, problems in the West Side community were not solved.

Henry B.'s job as assistant juvenile probation officer of Bexar County threw him into the social misery of the West Side, where most of the city's Mexican Americans lived. He was assigned to handle all major felony offenses for boys and girls. He said his method was simple. "You work with the people, you go to the people, you live with them. You have to go to 'em. Lord Jesus Christ went among the sinners. He didn't mind letting the prostitutes rub elbows with him. He didn't sit on a swivel chair and do case work."[20]

Henry B. set the pattern for the rest of his life. He went to the people.

---

"He spoke out for people and the needs of the poor and working class long before it was easy to do. Henry B. was a catalyst for the advancement of the rights of Hispanics, people of color, and women."

—Ann Richards, former Texas governor

# CHAPTER 5

# ¡Ay! ¡Gonzalez!

Henry B.'s work as probation officer was dangerous, but he wouldn't carry a gun. He often chased "a fleeing boy over fences, through barking dogs, and squawking chickens."[1] He always caught his juvenile. Then, when he had outrun him, he would tell him he wasn't going to take him to the police. Much to the police's displeasure, he tended to take the side of the boy. "Life is trial and error," he said. "Nobody's given you a book. You're gonna make mistakes. I figured not half of one percent of them were really bad."[2]

One time, when he was shot at, Henry B. almost lost his pants. He was told to bring in a delinquent who had crawled through a car window and escaped. Dora Davenport, director of the probation section, was afraid the press would use the incident to prove that delinquents were out of control in San Antonio. She ordered Henry B. to bring in the boy by the next morning. About 2:00 A.M., he sneaked up to the West Side shack where the boy lived.

"I realized that I was trespassing ... but I get on the porch and I tiptoe and tiptoe. I go to the window where the light is. I see an older woman and a younger lady; she seemed to be

31

pregnant. I knew somebody else was in there. I came to this side—dark—tried to look in the window—couldn't see anything in there. I tiptoe again—to this day I'd swear it was a giant, six and a half feet, maybe seven feet tall. 'What are you doing here?' Somethin' was pressin' on me. 'You're not gonna take my little brother.' His hand was shakin'.

"I got hysterical—I grabbed his hand—I dug so deep that my fingernails cut into him a fourth of an inch. It musta been a hundred-year-old .45, a silver-like chamber—he had the hammer back. Goes off—I got powder burned—it hit my belt and cut it—my pants started slipping down to my ankles. He has his left arm across my Adam's apple, and as we started falling backward off the porch I thought, 'I'm gone.' As we're going back I feel what seemed like a blast of air—we land. I still hold on to him. The father, hearing and knowing what happened, was choking him to death. I get the gun, my pants down to here. I got it and threw it clear across the alley and a shack into the backyard. The father says, '¡Ay! ¡Gonzalez! ¡Perdon! ¡Perdon!' He knew me.

"Just then the boy I was looking for came up to the house with a girl. '¡Ay! ¡Gonzalez!' He runs right through the house and through the window at the back and cuts himself all up, his arms, abdomen, side. I wrap him up and take him to my car—he messed up my back seat with his blood. More than forty stitches."[3] Henry B. did not do anything about the brother who attacked him. The next morning, the director of the probation section had the boy.

## Friend of Juvenile Delinquents

Henry B. often had to transport delinquents to Gatesville State Reform School. Sometimes he took them by his house for breakfast before they left San Antonio. One time he had three boys in his custody and stopped for breakfast and to pick up Bertha to ride with him. She fixed the meal and afterward asked one of the boys to take the trash to the alley. "Of course, he took off with Henry chasing him," she said.

Henry caught the boy and came back to the house. "What were you thinking?" he demanded.

"Well, I guess I wasn't" she said, laughing.[4] Henry B. didn't find anything funny about it, but he didn't report the incident to the police. He just didn't let the boys out of his sight again before he turned them over to an official at Gatesville.

That was the kind of thing that made him popular on the West Side, where he spent a lot of time. People liked and respected him. He had a reputation as tough but fair. Every large family had dealt with Henry B. one way or another. He had either helped keep a family member out of jail or helped put him or her in jail.

## First Mexican American Chief Probation Officer

County Judge Charles Anderson appointed Henry B. chief probation officer in 1946, making him the first Mexican American chief of a public agency in San Antonio in the twentieth century. He had already started the casework method of dealing with juveniles and their families. He created a new rule: Before a juvenile was taken before a court, a case worker had to visit the youth's home. An Anglo case worker in the office, who had told the judge that she didn't like working under a Mexican, disagreed with the new rule. "No decent white woman would be caught dead out on the West Side," she told Henry B.

"I could take offense," he replied, "because my mother lives on the West Side, and you are not superior to her."[5] Within several months, the case worker was successfully working with Mexican American girls.

African Americans were concentrated on the East Side. There was little help for black youths in trouble. The police didn't care if an African American juvenile was brought in or not, as long as the offense was on the East Side. A volunteer case worker in Henry B.'s office was a graduate of a school of social work. She was African American, and Judge Anderson told Henry B. he could let her work in an office on the East Side, but not in the courthouse. Henry B. resigned. The judge backed down and asked Henry B. to stay.

## Defends "Punks"

Judge Anderson sent Henry B. a sixty-seven-year-old political appointee who made the mistake of letting Henry B. hear him call the boys they were working with "punks." Anderson insisted Henry B. use the man, and Henry B. once again resigned. "If I do not have the right to hire and fire, I am not interested in the position," Henry B. told Judge Anderson.[6] That time, his resignation stuck. The controversy with Judge Anderson left Henry B. with a dislike for politicians. He was convinced that the issue was politically motivated. He had no political ambitions of his own. Henry B. later said that he considered his years as a probation officer to be the "most satisfying and most inspiring years and the ones that educated me, because those years were the equivalent of three or four college degrees."[7]

When Henry B. began his work with juveniles, Bexar County had more than a hundred boys in the state reform school at Gatesville. When he left there were six, and juvenile delinquency in the county had fallen by about a third.[8] But all that good work did not help Henry B. in his present condition. He and Bertha were expecting their fourth child, and Henry B. had no job. They gave up their house and furniture and moved into a duplex. "All I had," Henry B. related, "was books. So we made books into chairs. We put ice in a tub—that was our icebox."[9]

Henry B. accepted a job as executive secretary of the Junior Deputies of America. It was financed by the Kiwanis Club and was organized to work with delinquents. Money ran out, and he went to work as executive secretary of the Pan American Progressive Association (PAPA). He assisted people who were in need of better living conditions. He helped get water piped into one of the West Side slum sections. He was responsible for one of the major breakthroughs for Mexican Americans against discrimination in housing. He became active in fighting against restrictions in neighborhoods that barred Mexican Americans from purchasing property or building a home. Two influential members of the association's board made some ugly, racist remarks, and Henry B. resigned.

## Independent Businessman

Henry B. and Bertha had added another daughter to their family. Bertha was born in December 1947, making four children to support. "I decided," Henry B. said, "I could earn $300 a month on my own hook and not take all that baloney."[10] In 1948 he opened his own office in the Houston Building. He had a Spanish-English translation service and was a business consultant. He wrote for bicultural publications. He became educational director for the International Ladies Garment Workers Union and taught the members English and citizenship. He also taught mathematics at Sidney Lanier High School in the Veterans' Training Program. He did a variety of services for Mexican Americans, including writing letters for them. Frank Duane, a young man who had worked with Henry B., said, "He was about as close as you could get to the old-fashioned scribe working on the square in a Mexican town."[11]

He was active in religious and civic affairs. He served six years as scoutmaster of the Boy Scout troop at San Fernando Cathedral, although he had never been a scout himself. He served as president of the San Fernando Holy Name Society and as first president of the Bishop's committee for the Spanish speaking. He published *English and Spanish Review*, a magazine devoted to literary and social issues. The bilingual magazine did not make enough money to pay for itself. He stopped publication after five issues. Henry B. became very popular as a speaker for the Mexican American social clubs. By 1949, newspaper articles referred to him as a "San Antonio civic leader."[12]

## Political Influence

He became interested in the politics of the community. He was active in numerous Mexican American improvement organizations. He became aware of the influence that office holders had on policies affecting the poor, the uneducated, and the sick. He had overcome his shyness while working in the juvenile office, and he had a talent for making statements that newspaper reporters liked to use.

Between the years 1946 and his first election bid in 1950, Henry B. laid the groundwork for a political career.

---

"[Henry B.] was one of the rarest political characters I have ever known. And he was a champion for civil rights before we even knew what it was. . . . Henry did it his way. And he was as fearless in his crusading as he was right on most issues."

—J. J. "Jake" Pickle, former
Democratic congressman

# CHAPTER 6

# *Creeping Socialist*

In 1950 no one believed that a candidate of Mexican descent could win a countywide election in the San Antonio area. When Henry B. asked the city's Mexican American leaders to run for office, they told him he was crazy, that a Mexican could not win.[1] Often, Anglo politicians used money to buy the support of many Mexican Americans, but elections were won by candidates who received the majority of votes on the North Side. Only two Mexican Americans held elected offices in Bexar County—a justice of the peace and a constable. Poll taxes and indifference cut down the Mexican American vote. Everybody ran at-large, citywide or countywide. There was no Voting Rights Act. There was no such thing as a safe ethnic district. To raise money for a race was impossible. The handful of Mexican Americans who had money to give were totally opposed to anything that might "make the Americans mad."[2]

Henry B. asked Gus Garcia to run for the legislature in 1950. Garcia had been elected to a local education board. He was a charismatic Hispanic lawyer and had influence in the community. He told Henry B. that "a Mexican can't win

... and besides, it doesn't pay any money." (The legislature paid $5 a day for 120 days every other year.) When Henry B. pushed him to reconsider, Garcia shouted, "you're just an *encamidor.* You run yourself—leave me alone!"[3] Henry B. thought about it and decided he was in fact an *encamidor,* a goat that gets others to do it.

## Parents Disapprove of Political Career

His parents opposed Henry B. becoming involved in politics. Like others who were afraid of making people angry, his mother warned, "You'll make the Americans mad." His father was more emphatic with his disapproval. *"Eres un fracaso,"* said Leonides Gonzalez: "You are a disaster."[4] Leonides had many fears based on his own political experiences in Mexico. Also, Leonides always told his son, "We're Mexicans, and we're here as sojourners."[5] He would say, "I am grateful for the hospitality the United States has afforded. It has given me the protection of its laws. I will not immerse myself in their politics."[6] After being in the United States for forty years, Leonides still believed that his family was in the United States as guests and would return to their motherland. He was wrong.

Henry B. wanted to please his parents, but he was the rebellious child in the family. As a boy he had lived on the Anglo side of San Pedro Creek. "Cross the creek and you were on the West Side. That was *real* poverty. That was *real* hunger," he said.[7] He had crossed the creek often and had seen his relatives dying. Tuberculosis was common. One area was known as the Death Triangle, where there were more infant deaths than anywhere else in the country. He had watched his father's cousin's family all gradually die of tuberculosis. He wanted to make a difference in people's lives.

## First Political Campaign

He made up his mind. He was going to run for the legislature. In 1950 he hardly knew what a precinct was. He had to be told where to file for office. Maury Maverick Jr. described Henry B.'s situation as "running barefoot," because he had no money.[8] He spent $270 in the campaign, $70 of it on his filing fee. He paid $60 to a union printing shop for 2,000 bumper stickers, 100 placards, and 50,000 handcards. He worked day and night until he had given away all 50,000 of them. He based his campaign on an urgent need for "real and true" representation for the "common citizen—the wage earner."[9] People knew him as an honest, conscientious, dynamic, intelligent man. They rallied to support him: grocers, schoolteachers, parents of juveniles he had helped, former juveniles who had reached voting age, and fellow members of the Lions' Club, the Eagles, and the Organized Voters League.

He won in the runoff and was teamed up with Maury Maverick Jr., who was running for another seat in the countywide election. Maverick was the son of Maury Maverick Sr., the former New Deal congressman from San Antonio. Maverick Sr. went to work to create a Maverick-Gonzalez partnership in the runoff. Henry B. and the Mavericks agreed to cooperate in a unified effort to get the two men elected. Henry B. lost by 2,000 votes. Maverick Jr. won by 600 votes because both the North Side and the West Side had supported him. The Anglos in the North Side had not supported Henry B. In his victory speech, Maverick Jr. said,

40

"I attribute my victory to Henry B. Gonzalez as much as to any other man in Bexar County." He sent a telegram to Gonzalez in which he said: "It has been an honor to be associated with you because you are a brave and first-rate man."[10]

The day after the election, Maverick Sr. took Henry B. to lunch at the St. Anthony Hotel. The place was filled with local businessmen. Maverick said in a loud voice, "These are the people who voted against you and Maury Junior," He also told Henry B., "I want to talk to you before you get bitter . . . I don't want you to be bitter. You need a job. They need a man over at the Housing Authority."[11] Henry B. and Bertha had just added their third son, Steven, to their family in February 1951. With five children and a wife to support, Henry B. did, indeed, need a job.

He accepted the job with the Housing Authority. The agency was building public housing, but people were being dispossessed from their slum homes. Henry B. was the man needed for family relocation. He relocated 455 families without one eviction. He was appointed the first manager of Mirasol Homes, a public housing project in the far west of the city. He served there until he decided to run for city council in 1953. His father was furious. *"¡Estas perdiendo tiempo!"* he told his son. *"Eres un fracaso."* "You're wasting your time. You are a catastrophe, a failure."[12]

## First Mexican-American on City Council

City officials were divided into two groups in 1953. There were the San Antonians and the Citizens Committee, both trying to capture city hall. The San Antonians were against the out-of-towner city manager who had been hired by the Citizens Committee and decided that they needed a Mexican name on the ballot to get support from the West Side. The West Side was usually ignored, but the San Antonians knew they could not win without the Mexican-American votes. Henry B. was already known by everyone on the West Side. They liked and respected him. His main issue was getting a court of domestic relations for Bexar County, which was not an ethnic issue. The San Antonians put Henry B. on their slate. He won without a runoff. The San Antonians defeated the Citizens Committee and promptly elected Jack White mayor and Henry B. mayor pro-tem.

It wasn't long before they regretted their decision. At his first council meeting, Henry B. opposed a water-rate increase. Then the prominent businessmen behind the San Antonian group called a secret council meeting to discuss city appointments. The businessmen warned the council members that only the mayor was allowed to talk to the press. Henry B. ignored the warning and promptly answered a reporter's questions. A few days later, a businessman called Henry B. and offered him a well-paid job. Henry B. turned it down. Another meeting was held in the home of a councilman, but the businessman was missing. Henry B. asked where he was and was told by the councilman's wife, "I don't let Jews in my home." Henry B. walked out. "I felt," he recalled, "surrounded by ignorance."[13]

Henry B. worked full-time on council business. The pay was dismal—$20 a meeting and no more than $1,040 a year to live on. He continued his translation business but had constant interruptions from his constituents. He and his family lived very frugally. "There were no luxuries; everyone worked," said Henry B. Jr. He described the family as "circling the covered wagons" around Henry B., who was "considered the family's Martin Luther King."[14] Henry B. relied heavily on help from his father, his brother Joaquin, and loans.

## Meeting the Press

During his three years as a city councilman, Henry B. became a press personality. When the mayor and city manager suggested burning "Communist-tinged" books in the public library, Henry B. fought against it. He said he didn't favor "labeling, much less burning books ... particularly when the burning smells of Hitler tactics."[15] His name became a household word as he fulfilled a "self-dedicated" mission of "protecting the minority in matters of culture as well as economy."[16]

He was headline news when he told of an attempted bribe to keep him quiet about vice problems in San Antonio. He was in statewide news when he and his family were denied use of Camp Warnecke, a swimming and picnic area in New Braunfels, because they were Mexican Americans. "I thought we were told to leave because my bathing suit was so ugly," said Rose Mary, whose birthday the family was celebrating.[17] His critics accused him of "headline hunting." He answered them by quoting Charles Péguy, a French philosopher: "He who failed to bellow the truth when he knew the truth is an accomplice of liars and cheats."[18]

Some of his critics attacked with more deadly intent. He was shot at on three different occasions after making controversial statements in the press. He, Bertha, and another couple were returning to San Antonio from Castroville one night around nine o'clock. Someone drove past them and shot through their windshield. No one was hit, but it could have been deadly. One night as Henry B. and Bertha were going into their house after a social evening, someone went through the alley, shooting as fast as their gun would fire. Bertha was scratched and bruised from Henry B. pushing her down to keep her from being hit.

Another time, Bertha heard Henry B. coming up on the porch. Then she heard a shot. She waited for him to come into the house. After what seemed like hours, he didn't come in, so Bertha went outside to look for him. He was waiting in the dark for the car to come back so he could get the license number.

The Gonzalez family never called attention to where they lived. They told the children not to say who their father was. "It was scary," said Bertha, "but we didn't worry about the children, because they worked all over the place and no one knew who they were."[19]

Some of the businessmen who had supported the San Antonians were unhappy with Henry B. His statements about equality, water rates, and other issues were giving their opponents, the Citizens Committee, material for the next election. It was hinted that he could resign and find attractive employment outside city government. That only confirmed his decision to remain in office. He not only remained for the first term, but he decided to run a second term as an independent.

## Attacked by Enemies

Henry B.'s opponents attacked him every way they could. He was investigated for possible wrongdoing. When he was told that he was being investigated by police detectives, he said, "I'm the only damn politician, and Mexican especially, who never took money to campaign for anybody—never will and never have. If you come up with something it's a frame-up. What I cannot stand is a frame-up. I'm alone in politics. I don't have any money. All I have is my name and my family."[20] An enemy found a woman on the West Side who said Henry B. had pretended to be a lawyer and had taken money from her to defend her son. The *San Antonio Light* printed the woman's story, in which she accused Henry B. of practicing law without a license.

Henry B. called it a lie. He told his enemy that he had better not let the sun set on the lie, because he'd kill him if he did. He was kept from hunting the man by an urgent call from Bertha, who was still weak from a breech delivery of their sixth child, Genevieve, who was born in February 1953. When Bertha heard the accusation on the radio, she went to bed with a high fever. Henry B. had to go home to take care of her and his children. "That's what kept me from makin' a fool of myself," he later said.[21] A *San Antonio Express* reporter tracked down the woman and she admitted the story was not true. She said that she didn't even know Henry B. This story ran in the daily newspaper, clearing his name.

Henry B. was working long hours, and the pay was almost nothing. Bertha threatened him, "Either you get out or I'm getting out," she told him. "I don't know where I would have gone," she continued. "I had six children and no way to support myself."[22] Bertha was expecting their seventh child, Frank, who was born in June 1954. Until the false-accusation incident, Henry B. had planned to quit. Now he decided on the spot to run for a second council term. He realized that he was in a heated and dangerous

45

campaign, though, when he was shot at one night as he entered his home. He decided to remain quiet about the shooting so as not to influence voters. There was no need for concern; he won by almost 2,000 votes over his four opponents. And his 1955 reelection was won by the votes of the North Side.

During his years as a councilman, Henry B. spoke out against segregation. In early 1956 he proposed ordinances desegregating all city facilities, and the council passed them. He called for a tax-rate reduction. He opposed water-rate hikes unless the need was fully investigated. About public utilities he said they "stand apart from private business and in exchange for the monopoly they enjoy, must submit to regulation and reflect the public's interest."[23]

## Rebel Runs for State Senator

On his fortieth birthday, May 3, 1956, Henry B. announced his candidacy for state senator. He said that many of the state's crucial problems "have been postponed too long" and that "some action must be taken" on them.[24] The mayor thanked him for his help and inspiration. His fellow councilmen expressed their appreciation for his work, which had helped all San Antonians. "He was such a rebel in city council that John Daniels and others ... were so glad to get rid of him that they paid his filing fee for office," laughed Bertha. "They raised the whole $100 filing fee among themselves!"[25] Also, Henry B. was as poor as ever. "I couldn't even get $1.98 to buy shoes at Solo Serve for my little kid," he told a reporter.[26] But he had overcome one obstacle. He was reconciled with his parents, and they supported him in his campaign for senator.

Henry B.'s opponent was the incumbent Senator O. E. "Ozzie" Latimer, a Democrat. Latimer was not an outstanding campaigner, but he was experienced and settled in his post. In the six years that Henry B. had run for a seat in the House of Representatives and served as city councilman, he had become an astute politician. He had a commitment to the public that no one else seemed to have. He studied and mastered city budget procedures. He listened to and attempted to help his constituents.

Henry B. felt qualified to serve in the State Senate, but he didn't think he could win. He was a liberal Democrat. Latimer was a conservative who had been supported financially by the business community. In the 1952 presidential election, the county had voted for Republican Dwight Eisenhower. Most political forecasters predicted the same outcome for the 1956 election. It was going to be an uphill battle, and he had no funds for his campaign. He also had one other handicap. He was Mexican American.

He campaigned day and night. He relied on volunteers to distribute materials and on testimonial dinners to raise funds. He used television sparingly but effectively. Interest on the West Side and South Side grew, but he knew he had to have the North Side Anglo votes to win the primary. He campaigned as an independent. He did not ask for endorsement of interest groups. Latimer was confident that he would carry the North Side, which would offset votes for Henry B. on the South Side and West Side.

## First Elected Mexican-American State Senator

Henry B. won the primary by 282 votes. His victory was called a "staggering upset against long odds" and was credited to his "personality and relentless drive."[27] As soon as he was announced the winner of the primary, the Republican Party of Bexar County announced that a Republican would oppose him in the general election. The party chose Jesse Oppenheimer, who admitted that if Latimer had won the primary, the Republicans would not have entered a candidate.

The campaign was bitter and sensational. Henry B. charged that the interests that backed Democrat Latimer were now backing his Republican opponent. He accused Latimer's backers of ganging up on him, since he was the only one with an opponent. Henry B. understood that Oppenheimer had called him a communist. When he confronted Oppenheimer, the Republican said all he had called Henry B. was "a left-wing, creeping socialist." Henry B. replied that he was a right-handed pitcher and therefore a "right-winger." He said that the only thing "creeping" about him were his "shorts."[28] Oppenheimer repeatedly warned the voters of the dangers of electing a liberal such as Henry B. Henry B. answered with his own definition of a liberal. "I mean by liberal, a man who believes in living and letting live, in toleration, a person not dogmatic. If that's what liberal means, I'm proud to be called one."[29]

All of Henry B.'s work paid off. He won the general election to become the first elected Mexican American state senator in Texas history. (In 1846 Antonio Navarro, a native Texan of Spanish-Italian descent, was appointed state senator and served one term.) Everyone was surprised, because Republican Dwight Eisenhower carried Bexar County by a greater margin than in 1952. It was the reverse of the coat-tail theory that voters tend to vote for the party of a popular president. The *San Antonio Light* called his victory "a just reward for worthy public service."[30]

Henry B.'s first political victory was only the beginning of his lifelong victories representing the people of the 20th Congressional District.

---

"In 1939, 53 percent of the citizens of [San Antonio] lived in substandard housing, and 68 percent of the Mexican Americans had incomes of less than $550 a year. In 1945 one in twenty local Hispanics had tuberculosis; in '46, Hispanic children accounted for two-thirds of all the infant deaths in [San Antonio].[31]

# CHAPTER 7

# *That Mexican*

"I'm not going to have that Mexican represent me in Austin," Henry B. overheard a woman lawyer say. She was surprised to hear him answer, "Relax, lady, you have him."[1] Many Bexar County citizens were shocked when Henry B. was elected state senator. There was disbelief in Republican circles that a "Mexican" was now their representative. The same attitude was carried over in Austin, where some senators and state officials referred to him as "that Mexican."[2] Henry B. had heard it all before, and he had overcome it. He could do it again.

Henry B. cut a dashing figure in the ornate Texas Senate. He often wore a white suit and white shoes that set him apart from the conservatively dressed senators. He first learned the rules and customs of the Senate.

The Senate was made up of a group of very conservative and clubby members. They were often open to bribery and frequently mean-spirited. In the Senate, issues were frequently determined by personalities and special or personal interests. Tony Korioth, elected to the House in 1956, recalled, "Segregation bills were passing the House like a rocket. Being a member of the NAACP was a felony. I had never seen hate like that. It was just pure hate that didn't make sense."[3] They did respect a man of intelligence, logic, and manners. Henry B. had come from an aristocratic background and had all of those qualities, but he had to earn their respect.

He was at home in the Senate. He liked rough-and-tumble political battles. He was told that forcing integration on Texas would bring trouble for African Americans. Henry B. replied, "Falling out of bed means nothing if you're already sleeping on the floor." His opponents charged that he was unstable. Henry B. responded, "What they mean is that they can't tell me what to do. And when they say I am financially irresponsible, they mean I would rather remain poor than sell out."[4]

He won passage of a bill letting cities start slum clearance programs. He introduced a bill for a 40-cent-per-hour minimum wage which never had a hearing. The Texas Employers' Association called him "a radical" because he fought for the poor.[5] He introduced the strongest lobbyist control measure proposed during that period. It had no chance to pass. Lobbyists would have gladly paid his bills for an apartment in Austin, but he commuted daily between San Antonio and Austin. During the 1950s, that meant four or five hours of driving each day.

## Longest Filibuster in Texas History

In the political climate of the 1950s, oratory skills could pass or kill a bill up for vote. Henry B. had those skills. In 1954 the U.S. Supreme Court ruled in *Brown v. Board of Education* that schools had to desegregate. Texas was one of the southern states that tried to get around the law. Texas legislators tried to pass laws that would keep public schools segregated in spite of the ruling. Texas Governor Price Daniel, of Liberty, in East Texas, supported the racists. The first of ten bills passed the House and was sent to the Senate for vote. Henry B. and Senator Abraham "Chick" Kazen of Laredo had warned that they would filibuster any segregation bill to come before the Senate. When word spread that there was to be a filibuster to try to defeat the bill, Governor Daniel said to Henry B., "Henry, you're not gonna fight our nigger bills, are ya?" Henry B. replied, "Well, Governor, you just give me the floor, and I'll do the rest."[6]

Kazen gained the floor of the Senate and began a fifteen-hour filibuster. The bill allowed placement of schoolchildren for reasons other than color. It included a provision for mental agility tests to be given to determine student placement. Kazen pointed out the flaws of the bill and shamed the legislature for attempting to ignore the "law of the land."[7] He was helped by questions asked by Henry B. and a few other friendly senators. When Kazen began to tire, Henry B. took the floor.

Henry B. paced around his desk. He was dressed in a light blue suit, yellow tie, yellow pocket handkerchief, yellow socks, and white athletic shoes. "Why did they name Gonzales *Gonzales* if the name wasn't honored in Texas at the time?" he asked. "Why did they honor Garza along with Burnet? My own forebears in Mexico bore arms against Santa Anna. There were three revolutions against Santa Anna. Texas was only one of its manifestations! Did you know Negroes helped settle Texas? That a Negro died at the Alamo?"[8]

Hour after hour he spoke, without notes to help him.

He quoted Herodotus, Jeremiah, Shakespeare, and others from memory. He read from Lord Macauley's 1831 statement on the civil disabilities of Jews and a passage from W.E.B. DuBois in *An Anthology of Negro Literature*. Senator Wardlow Lane of Center, Texas, was the segregationists' floor leader. He grumbled about Henry B.'s big words. "Maybe he'll strangle on one of them," he said hopefully.[9] The Senate gallery filled and stayed filled all through the night. Once it was emptied as a penalty for applause, but it filled again. To the argument that integration would lead to intermarriage among African Americans and Anglos, Henry B. said, "They want to be your brothers, not your brothers-in-law."[10]

He told of his experiences as a member of a minority group. He said the bill could be used against Mexican Americans as well as African Americans. He asked whether Texas liberty was only the liberty of Anglo-Saxons. *Time* magazine reported that "time and again he warned his colleagues of the ultimate perils of segregation. 'It may be some can chloroform their conscience. But if we fear long enough, we hate, and if we hate long enough, we fight.'"[11]

The filibuster, which lasted thirty-six hours and two minutes, kept the Senate in session for the longest continuous period in Texas history. Henry B. talked twenty-one hours and two minutes before the Senate agreed to drop the other segregation bills if he would just stop talking and agree to that one bill. Almost every newspaper in Texas reported the filibuster on their front pages with banner headlines. National magazines and news commentators reported the Kazen-Gonzalez talkathon. Ann Richards, later governor of Texas, said of the filibuster, "One of the most impassioned filibusters I have ever heard. ... He delivered the notion that no matter what the Texas legislature said or did, these bills if made into law would be unconstitutional. Henry stopped the wholesale passage of these bills into law and was ultimately proved right. The Texas Supreme Court subsequently ruled all of them unconstitutional."[12] His uncompromising stand on segregation lifted him into statewide prominence.

## Disagreement with Governor Daniel

Henry B. received the state NAACP Citizenship Award. He was named the outstanding Latin American Citizen of the Year by the Alba Club of the University of Texas. He accepted speaking engagements all over the state. Newspapers referred to him as "liberal Senator Gonzalez."

Henry B.'s disagreements with Governor Daniel kept him in the news. Henry B. opposed the appointment of Joe Frazier Brown to the judgeship of the new 150th District Court. The court would handle matters involving juvenile and domestic cases involving children. Daniel appointed Brown to the judgeship without consulting Henry B., which was senatorial custom. Henry B. opposed Brown's appointment.

During the controversy, many papers predicted that Henry B. had placed his political career in jeopardy. He would not give in to pressure. He said he would not "abandon the office to accept the views of anyone else" and added, "Some people think *they* are the Senator from Bexar County."[13] When Brown's judgeship was defeated, one San Antonio reporter wrote that "although a lot of people can't quite get used to the idea, Gonzalez is starting to insist on being treated like a senator."[14] Another headline read, "Daniel Finds Gonzalez Can't Be Pressured."[15]

The second fight with Governor Daniel was over the "Troop bill." The bill would give the governor authority to close schools where there was a threat of violence and the possibility of federal troops being called in. Gonzalez filibustered against the bill for twenty hours. He accused Daniel of seeking powers to make himself "czar of school districts."[16] Daniel went on statewide television in support of the "Troop bill" and denounced Henry B.'s stand. The bill passed, but again Henry B. had called attention to the segregation issue.

He also had called unwanted attention to himself. Someone drove by his home and shot a gun; fortunately, the bullet hit the foundation of the house and no one was hurt. He received threatening phone calls, and people came up to him on the street and in restaurants and made threats. He also received hate mail, but he didn't let any of it influence his votes or support of bills.

## The Long Commute to Austin

The long commute from San Antonio to Austin each day during the legislative session took its toll on family life. "People don't understand that when you filibuster you have a bad, bad case of just a raw throat. Dad would come home in a total state of exhaustion. If we had something we wanted to talk to him about, it just wasn't going to happen. He couldn't talk, he was so tired," Charlie said of his father. "I remember him just crawling upstairs to go to bed and having to rest before he could eat."[17]

One time young Bertha asked her mother, "Where is Daddy?"

Her mother said, "He is in Austin. Why do you ask that?"

Bertha replied, "Well, I never see him."

Henry B. left the house before she got up in the morning and arrived back home after she had gone to bed at night. "You had better go in there and say hello to your daughter. She thinks that you don't live here anymore," Bertha told Henry B.[18]

Most of the time Bertha saw that the children were dressed and ready for school. One morning Henry B. took over. He had a loud, gruff voice, and he was yelling, "Get ready! You are going to be late. Hurry! Hurry!" Five-year-old Bertha stopped, put her hands on her hips, looked her father in the eye, and said, "Hey, I'm no dog. You don't talk to the dog that way!" Henry B. laughed, but he didn't do it again.[19]

Henry B. and Bertha's eighth and last child, Anna, was born in September 1958. The older children helped Bertha with the younger ones. Henry Jr. was very mature for his age and accepted the responsibility without complaint. Rose Mary carried a pencil and paper around to take notes. "They ruled with an iron hand," Bertha laughed. "Are you going to be a schoolteacher?" she asked Rose Mary. (Rose Mary did become a schoolteacher.) "I never said 'Wait until your daddy comes!' to discipline the children," Bertha said and added, "The children said, 'We get along okay with Mother, but don't cross her up!'"[20]

Bertha and the children were always ready to go camping when Henry B. had the time. Their favorite place was Padre Island. Bertha made each child a quilted, zippered pillowcase in different colors and patterns. Each child had a towel, swimming trunks, t-shirt, clean set of clothes, toothbrush, and comb. One large duffel bag contained "community" things that everyone used. Those things stayed packed all the time. As soon as they came home from a campout, everything was washed and replaced in the pillowcase. When Henry B. came home and said, "Let's go!," everyone was ready to jump into the car and head for Padre Island.[21]

## Campaign for Governor

In 1958 the Democratic Party tried to find a candidate for the governor's race. Henry B. agreed to run for the office, although there was little hope for success. Governor Price Daniel, the incumbent, was running for a second term in office. Henry B. was Mexican American, a liberal, and a Catholic. He argued that every candidate should be forced to take stands on issues that other politicians avoided. Again, he attracted major news coverage that gave him an opportunity to discuss issues of importance to Texans.

Henry B. didn't accept large campaign contributions from individual sources. He didn't want the strings that were attached to those donations. He also disliked "tickets" of candidates. "You become part of the pack. You are expected to go along to get along. I don't believe in that," he explained.[22] He spent only $17,000 in the race, whereas Daniel spent $90,000.[23]

He traveled over the state several times. Because he did not expect to win, he could speak out without worrying about offending voters. "I had no fear of losing and no false hope of winning," Henry B. said of the campaign. "I was able to express myself as my heart and mind dictated."[24] In his speeches he criticized Governor Price Daniel for his lack of leadership in state government. He said he supported federal aid for school lunches. He opposed a sales or state income tax. He called for state colleges and universities to do away with tuition so poor students could attend. He asked for a youth conservation program. He wanted a tax on natural gas pipelines. And in all sections of Texas, he called for an end to segregation.

He was accepted as a major candidate and was given news coverage as he drove around the state in a second-hand station wagon. But Daniel received 60 percent of the vote. Henry B. had 19 percent of the vote and carried eleven counties. While it was not enough to win the election, some observers concluded that Mexican American voters were entering a new political phase. The election served another purpose. When Henry B. returned to Austin for the regular session of the 57th Legislature, he was no longer referred to as "that Mexican." Even his political opponents greeted him warmly.[25]

## Fights for San Antonio

Six members of Bexar County's delegation in the House were conservatives and often did not agree with Henry B. But he was able to work with them to pass a medical school bill that ended a twelve-year struggle. The bill passed despite opposition from Senator Charles Herring, who wanted the Health Science Center to be built in Austin instead of San Antonio. Henry B. fought to delete the taxing section from a bill to establish the Edwards Underground Water District and to require that its board of directors be elected rather than appointed. He opposed the creation of new taxing bodies. The San Antonio River Authority (SARA) asked for the power to levy taxes to raise necessary money to continue flood-control projects. In explaining his opposition to the bill, he said, "The small homeowners here not only are threatened by a flood of water but by a flood of tax lien foreclosures which would force these people out of their homes."[26]

Henry B. was effective in his role as an irritant in the Senate. He filibustered for four hours against changing the dates of primary elections from summer to spring. He predicted that the bill would create difficulties if it passed without study. Governor Daniel threatened to veto the bill unless the conflicting and confusing sections were not changed. The bill was corrected and passed the Senate. Henry B. was given credit with being "either the smartest or the luckiest politician in a long time" because of his predictions.[27] When conservative colleagues suggested that Henry B. should not be so verbal and critical, his answer was: "I wasn't elected to this office by any members of the Senate. I was elected by the citizens of Bexar County, and they are the only ones I owe anything to."[28]

## "One good term deserves another"

Invitations to speak in all parts of the state and in Colorado, California, Kansas, Michigan, and other places kept Henry B. on the move. He reported to his constituents by television in both Spanish and English. Paul Thompson, a *San Antonio News* reporter, wrote that Henry B.'s "colorful phrases, impish humor and deft jabs at the critical have endeared him to multitudes." He concluded that if Henry B. were not stopped in the next election, "no telling how big he can grow or what bauble he can snatch."[29]

Henry B. announced that he would run for another term in the State Senate. Four other Democrats announced themselves as candidates for his seat, including "Ozzie" Lattimer, whom he had defeated in 1956. The 1960 elections were charged with excitement. Lyndon Baines Johnson was going to bid for the Democratic nomination for presidency. A coalition of labor, minority representatives, independent liberals, and others organized for a major effort in the primaries. It was an intensive and long campaign. Henry B. asked for reelection with the slogan "One good term deserves another."[30]

The primary election put Henry B. into a runoff with R. L. "Bob" Strickland, a businessman. Strickland ran a well-financed, hard-hitting campaign against Henry B. He tried to tie Henry B. to "union bosses." He ran a full-page ad in newspapers, warning voters of Henry B.'s union ties and pleading: "Don't Let Hoffa and Gonzalez Ruin Our State."[31] His campaign did not succeed. Henry B. was nominated as the Democratic candidate by a large majority.

Henry B. ran against Republican Ike Kampmann in the general election. Kampmann was a local attorney whose wife was a major officer in the state Republican Party. Henry B. was confident he could win. He didn't spend as much time on his own campaign as he did campaigning for John F. Kennedy for president. He campaigned in eleven states for Kennedy and the Democratic ticket. He was national co-chairman of the Viva Kennedy Clubs.

Henry B. defeated Kampmann easily, but the political power in Texas was beginning to shift. A number of conservative Democrats who had once controlled party politics in Texas were unhappy with Kennedy, Henry B., and other legislators with liberal views. These disgruntled Democrats switched to the Republican Party.

Henry B. continued to serve his constituents in the 20th

Congressional District, regardless of race, economic standing, or political party.

---

"I seek to register the plaintive cry, the hurt feelings, the silent, the dumb protest of the inarticulate . . ."

—Henry B. Gonzalez, filibustering
against segregation bills

# CHAPTER 8

# *The Irritant*

John F. Kennedy and Lyndon B. Johnson won the 1960 election. When Johnson became vice president, he had to resign from the U.S. Senate. His Senate seat was to be filled by a special election. Henry B. and Maury Maverick Jr. were discussed as possible candidates. But they knew that if they both ran for the same congressional seat, they would split the liberal vote and reduce the chance for either of them to win.

There was a misunderstanding between the two friends, however. Henry B. understood that if he announced his candidacy, Maverick wouldn't enter his name. Maverick believed that Henry B. had told him that if Maverick announced his candidacy, Henry B. would drop out of the race. Once they had both declared their candidacy, neither would back out. Both men ran for the seat in the U.S. Senate, and both lost.[1]

Liberal and moderate votes were divided, and Republican John Tower and conservative Democrat William Blakely led the race. Henry B. had a little less than 10 percent of the total vote, but he was first in Bexar

County, with 6,000 votes more than John Tower, the winner. The *San Antonio Light* reported that "once again [Bexar County voters] made it clear that State Senator Henry Gonzalez commands the largest and most loyal personal following of any local politician."[2]

The Sunday before the presidential inauguration, in January 1961, Henry B. received a personal call from President-elect John F. Kennedy. Kennedy offered to appoint Henry B. ambassador to a Latin American country. The country was not named and would be determined after the president consulted with Dean Rusk, secretary of state. Henry B. was very pleased by the offer but did not hesitate to refuse it. He confided to Kennedy that he preferred to campaign for the U.S. Senate, and, if he lost, to serve out his term as state senator. He said, "My ambitions are in the legislative field, not in diplomatic circles."[3]

## Campaign for U.S. Representative

Two months after Henry B. lost the Senate election, President Kennedy appointed Bexar County Congressman Paul J. Kilday to the Court of Military Appeals. Henry B. was the logical Democratic candidate to replace Kilday. He began campaigning again. His campaign headquarters distributed thousands of leaflets that emphasized, "in electing a U.S. Representative for Bexar County, experience and training count. ... Henry Gonzalez has the experience that makes him the trained man for you to send to Washington."[4]

It was the first congressional campaign since Kennedy's election and was depicted as a test of the president's New Frontier program. *Time,* the *Washington Post,* and other major publications closely followed the campaign. President Kennedy endorsed Henry B., and Robert Kennedy toured Texas with him. Vice President Johnson not only endorsed Henry B.'s candidacy, he teamed with a famous Mexican comedian, Cantinflas, to barnstorm for Henry B. during the final days of the campaign. Acting House Speaker Carl Albert and U.S. Representative Jim Wright came in to help campaign. Many of Henry B.'s State Senate colleagues and Governor Price Daniel joined his supporters.

When Henry B. began campaigning on a national level, politics heated up. His family became very sensitive to the criticism. "It was one thing when he was attacked on political issues or something. We learned to live with those kinds of criticism," said Charlie Gonzalez, "but when it got personal, it did hurt the family. And when your parent is ridiculed or demeaned, it is painful for a child."[5] When Henry B. was running for Congress, his opponent put a full-page ad in the newspaper with the Marines lifting the American flag on Iwo Jima during World War II. He gave his service record and listed his decorations. Then the question was asked, "Where was Henry B. during the war?"[6]

Sixteen-year-old Charlie had romanticized the Marines and the war, but he had never thought of his father's part in it. It bothered him that his father was being portrayed as a coward. He was waiting for his father in the kitchen at 1:00 A.M. one night when Henry B. came home from campaigning. He didn't say hello to his father but blurted out, "So, Dad, where *were* you during the war?"[7] As tired and hungry as he was, Henry B. took time to explain about his part in World War II. "There aren't many children whose parents' shortcomings or strengths are constantly reviewed publicly or in as much detail as the life of a political figure," Charlie said. "Sometimes during election day you are in a constant state of anxiety. But as a family, we just had to do our parts."[8]

## Another Victory

Henry B.'s opponent was John Goode, a lawyer and Bexar County Republican chairman. Goode considered himself a conservative. He had the endorsement of former president Dwight D. Eisenhower. Eisenhower had been stationed at Fort Sam Houston. He had coached high school and college football in San Antonio. He had married his wife in San Antonio and was well loved in Bexar County. Eisenhower had carried Bexar County in both the 1952 and 1956 presidential elections. Eisenhower did little good for his candidate, though. He mispronounced Goode's name during his endorsement speech.

On November 4, 1961, Henry B. Gonzalez was elected United States representative from the 20th District of Texas. Election results showed that there had been more interest in the campaign than in any other special election in Bexar County history. Over 90,000 votes were cast, more than in any similar election. Henry B. won by 10,000 votes. He was the first Texan of Mexican descent to win that honor. In explaining his victory, he said, "It's important to get out and meet voters and work hard at it for years, because you can't stereotype or pigeonhole humans, much as political leaders might like to."[9] He saw each voter as an individual and respected individual characteristics. He did not take voters for granted. He worked hard to include the North Side, but he did not forget the West Side.

## Setting Up Office in Washington

The first thing Henry B. had to do as a new congressman was to organize and set up his offices. He hired Gail Beagle to interview prospects and to establish his offices in Washington and San Antonio. Beagle first met Henry B. in 1958 when he was running for governor. She had just graduated from Texas Woman's University at Denton with a degree in journalism. She had borrowed $100 on her life insurance policy to go to Austin to look for a job. She used $10 of the money to go to a fundraiser for Henry B. at the Spanish Village in Austin. Beagle's parents resided in Nederland, Jefferson County, where she was living until she got a job. She asked Henry B., "Who is your Jefferson County campaign chairman?" He said, "No one. You can be my campaign manager."[10]

Beagle had no experience in running a political campaign, but she did it. When he lost the bid for governor, she worked for him as senator. The legislature met only every other year, and she had to find employment in Austin between sessions. When Henry B. ran for U.S. representative in 1961, she worked for him again as volunteer press aide. Her Austin employer was a Democrat and allowed her time to do both jobs. She moved to San Antonio during the campaign because Henry B.'s headquarters were there.

Each congressman was allotted twenty-two staff members. Those were divided between Washington and home offices. After Henry B. was elected to the U.S. Congress, Beagle hired people to work in his San Antonio office before moving to Washington to set up an office there. Henry B.'s sister Luz Tamez joined the staff in the San Antonio office, where she worked for twenty-nine years.

Henry B. chose to use fewer staff members in both offices so he could pay his Washington staff more; living expenses were much higher there than in San Antonio. They also had to work longer hours. Most of his staff came from San Antonio. Beagle made contacts through the local colleges and universities and was able to hire professional personnel who could make decisions and keep the offices running smoothly.

## First Mexican American Congressman

Henry B. was often asked what it was like to be the first Mexican American elected to Congress. "I was something of a curiosity being the only ethnic minority member in my delegation," he said. "I was a peer, but that was not to say I felt unwelcomed. And I stand before you today, accepted, but seen by some as an inconvenient and unwelcomed obstacle."[11]

He took his job as congressman seriously. He did a methodical and thorough study of legislative proposals on which he had to vote. He wanted to understand the proposals, as well as their possible consequences. He was often the lone voice to disagree or question in the Senate, because he was often the only truly informed member. He called upon his prior experiences and knowledge to clarify or explain a legislative proposal and its consequences.

Henry B. was idealistic, yet he was practical. He believed that the public good had to come before special interests. He did not accept money from groups or factions for campaign purposes and did not allow them to pressure him for support in Congress. He said, "I have to run as an independent, because that's the way I'm built; tickets are not good for the general public."[12] While he was a strict party man, he did not let the Democratic Party dictate his responsibility to his constituents. From the time of his first elected office, he was often criticized for his independence.

Henry B. thrived on criticism. During his five years in the State Senate he had handled, co-sponsored, or introduced forty-two bills that became law, often without help from others. He often played the "devil's advocate" who questioned his opponents.[13] He had admirers as well as critics. In 1961 Senator William N. Patman wrote to Henry B., "No matter how urgent the cause you pleaded, you never marred your conduct by petty discourtesies, arrogant sarcasm, or mean misbehavior. . . . It always seemed rather that your convictions fed upon adversity, that your character strengthened upon opposition, and your eloquence flowered by exposure to the most trying circumstances."[14]

## A Freshman Congressman

New members of Congress, or freshman congressmen, were expected to be seen but not heard. Representative Gonzalez of the 20th District in Bexar County, Texas, disregarded that unspoken rule. His colorful dress made him stand out, and his large, booming voice could not be silenced. He became "the irritant" in the U.S. House of Representatives. From the moment he went into Congress, he spoke out loudly and clearly against the poll tax, a fee that had to be paid before a person could vote. It was begun in the South to keep poor people from voting, particularly African Americans. It affected poor Mexican Americans, Anglos, and anyone who could not afford to pay. He introduced a bill to abolish the poll tax. That bill became part of the landmark Voting Rights Act of 1965. Others in

Congress got the message: Don't expect silence from Representative Gonzalez from Texas!

Because he was so outspoken, he received hate mail and threats on his life. He had been in Congress less than a year when he received several pieces of hate mail. One was a picture of a telescopic lens on a rifle with the cross hairs taped over a newspaper picture of Henry B. The cross hairs were focused on his head. "Look at this, son," he said to Henry B. Jr. "Can you imagine anyone sending something like this?" In one letter the writer wrote that Henry B. "was a chili-eating Mexican that ought to go back to Mexico." He laughed and said to his son, "Gosh, I didn't know that I ate that much chili!"[15]

Henry B. worked for all of his constituents, but in his thirty-seven years in Congress, he spoke loudest for the poor in his congressional district and in the United States. In a long speech to Congress, he said, "Get out of Washington. Find out what the people are doing. See how they are living. Visit lines in unemployment offices. Visit the places where free food is passed out. Sit for a day in a juvenile court. Visit jails. Go to a national park and see how foresight and planning have saved our natural resources. It could do the same for human resources. Walk around slums and talk with the people who live in them. It is a sad fact, but many people who go to Europe won't drive three miles to see what it's like on the other side of town."[16]

## The People—Always First

Henry B. kept an active office in the Houston Building in downtown San Antonio. He felt it was important that his constituents know what he was doing. He also wanted them to know he was available to them. He wrote letters and made a weekly radio broadcast. He appeared on television to give spot reports. Wherever he went, he talked to his constituents and invited them to his office. Often he was stopped by troubled citizens who requested help or advice, and he tried to help them. He did not limit his availability to Mexican Americans. He cultivated Anglos' confidence by assisting those who asked for his help. His public stands against book burning, utilities rates increases, and sales tax, along with his sympathy for the underdog, won approval from all ethnic groups. His actions convinced voters that "my own career is an illustration that the walls of prejudice can crumble," because "you will be heard when you have something to offer."[17]

Henry B. not only heard the voices of his constituents, he heard the voices of others. He read that some people in a town in Costa Rica had tried to save the burning home of an American family, but they had no fire truck. They needed a tank truck with a pressure pump they could use without a fire hydrant or a city water system. Henry B. asked the State Department to look through their surplus property lists. They did not have such a truck. He remembered, though, that this was the same kind of truck used by Texas contractors. He called a friend, and within two hours they had found an extra fire truck. The Costa Ricans flew to San Antonio, picked up the truck, and drove it along the Pan-American highway to their town. "All of which only proves that the road is never long between friends," Henry B. said.[18]

## Duties of a Congressman

As congressman, Henry B. found that he had to perform several duties to serve effectively. His duties were divided between legislation and constituents. As a Democrat, Henry B. had certain party responsibilities. He was expected to support the Democratic administration, but that did not keep him from voting for what he believed was right. He became a watchdog over federal agencies, particularly the Federal Aviation Agency. He was responsible for educating and informing the public of facts and situations that they would not otherwise know. And as a politician, he was responsible to the voters for reelection.

Henry B. took all of his duties seriously. Many times he was the only "irritant" in a political world where lobbyists wrote the bills to be passed. Since he was in "no one's pocket," he had nothing to lose. He said, "I cannot serve two masters."[19] He chose to serve the 20th District of Bexar County—in essence, the people of the United States.

---

"[Henry B.] never varied his support for the downtrodden and justice for all people regardless of race, color, or creed."

—Representative Martin Frost,
Democrat from Dallas

# CHAPTER 9

# *White Taco*

Soon after Henry B.'s election, he found himself at odds with the new generation of San Antonio's West Side Mexican American politicians. At first they sought his support. He would not fight the Good Government League (conservative Democrats) with them, join their ethnic political organizations, or take up causes like abolishing the Texas Rangers. He broke ties with Albert Peña, State Senator Joe Bernal, and State Representative Johnny Alaniz. Each fight was bitter and public.

Henry B.'s most vocal critics were the members of the Mexican American Youth Organization (MAYO). The group was headed by José Angel Gutiérrez, a student at St. Mary's University. Gutiérrez made a speech in 1969 in which he called for "the elimination of the gringo" by social or economic means and said, "If that doesn't work, we may have to resort to violence in self-defense."[1] Henry B. had already gone to the House Ways and Means Committee to attack MAYO's Ford Foundation funding. He accused MAYO of having a Cuban connection. MAYO denounced him as a "*vendido,* a *Tío Tomas,* a white taco, a traitor to his people."[2]

In spring 1970, Henry B. made a speech at St. Mary's University. A group staged a walkout. *"¡Vendido!"* they called him.

*"¡Pendejos!"* he called them.

They called him a sellout. He called them numbskulls.[3]

As the group of protesters began leaving, three students came up on the stage. There was some shoving and a couple of fists swung, but no one was hurt. Henry B. gave his speech.

There was another protest in 1973 at the University of Colorado in Boulder. Henry B. believed the same group that demonstrated at St. Mary's was behind it. About a dozen students took Henry B. into a room. One of the students said, "We demand that tonight you do not appear on the lecture platform unless you are prepared to denounce the gringo establishment and the mistreatment of Chicanos. ... You don't talk tonight unless you talk about Chicano rights. We're not requesting, we're demanding."[4] At first Henry B. was polite, but when he became very angry and began speaking in English and Spanish, the group left. As they were leaving, the student said, "All right, you better look out. Tonight we'll be back."[5]

At the auditorium building that night, there were picketers with signs that said, "Gonzalez, go home." The entrance was blocked by some of the young men who had been in the room with him. Henry B. said to the biggest one, *"Piojos, haganse a un lado, aqui viene su peine."* ("Lice, step aside, here comes your comb.")[6] Inside the auditorium there were about twenty demonstrators. One of the young men jumped onstage and tore out the microphone. As he raised his arm, Henry B. saw that he had a gun, and he looked around, realizing that several of the demonstrators

73

were armed and appeared to be on drugs. The professor in charge was accompanied by his wife. She pretended to faint. Henry B. and the professor pushed their way through the protesters with the wife held between them. They rushed to their car as the hecklers spat on them. Charges were filed against a student and the chairman of La Raza Unida Party of Colorado, but not against any Texans.

## More Local Criticism

Henry B. was also criticized by some San Antonio Catholic priests. Archbishop Robert E. Lucey said, "Oh, Henry Gonzalez has turned his back on the Mexican American." Henry B. responded with: "I have yet to see Archbishop Lucey in the shadow of Our Lady of Guadalupe on El Paso Street, and he lives in Hollywood Park [North Side], so who has turned his back on the West Side? The day I see Archbishop Lucey saying Mass in Our Lady of the Guadalupe, that day I'll listen to what he has to say about that."[7]

The Mexican American progressive movement came to a sad end as their leaders made charges and countercharges against one another. The younger Mexican American politicians said Henry B. did not want competition from others. They accused him of saying, "There is only one politician in this town, and that is me."[8] They pointed out that he had profited among Anglo conservatives by criticizing Mexican American activists. They called him "a big macho, a first-class macho."[9] When asked about the criticism, Henry B. said, "If I have achieved anything in Texas politics, it is to have established the idea that a minority politician can represent the whole community."[10] He told his critics, "Sooner or later I might have to make a decision, the organization versus my oath of office and my district. They think I'm trying to be a lone wolf or egotistical."[11]

## A Prophetic Congressman

Henry B. always visited the newspaper buildings when he was home from Washington, which was almost every weekend. He reported on what was going on in Washington and his opinion about it. One day he told a reporter, "Cuba is getting ready to attack the United States." The newsman thought to himself, "This time, he's gone too far."[12] That was just before the Cuban Missile Crisis. In the fall of 1962, the Soviet Union had begun setting up missile sites in Cuba and shipping in missiles. Despite President Kennedy's warning to the Soviets, aerial photographs showed missiles on decks of ships approaching Cuba. The United States ordered them to turn around and return to Russia.[13]

Lyndon Johnson described the tense situation: "As Kennedy and the leader of the Soviet Union came eyeball to eyeball, and their thumbs started inching up ... their thumbs started getting closer to that nuclear button, their knives were in each other's ribs almost ... and neither of them was flinching or quivering."[14] The Russians backed down. The Cuban crisis was one of many predictions made by Henry B. that proved true.

## Committee on Banking and Currency

Henry B.'s constituents had sent him to Washington with the hope that he would be appointed to the Armed Services Committee. San Antonians believed that if they did not have representation on the committee, San Antonio would lose some of its military bases. Henry B. did not gain a seat on that committee but was assigned to the Committee on Banking and Currency. He requested the assignment because it dealt with issues such as banking and international finance, and public housing and price controls, which affected all Americans. He had served on the Banking Committee in the State Senate. He had experience and interest in urban renewal, public housing, and consumer problems. But Henry B. didn't know what he was asking for when he requested the assignment. Likewise, the Committee on Banking and Currency didn't know what they were getting when he was assigned to the group. The committee had been passive, and Henry B. was anything but that.

He was disappointed with the Committee on Banking and Currency's inactivity. He became a close friend of Representative Wright Patman of Texarkana, Texas, who was also an activist. In 1963 Patman became chairman of the committee. He reorganized and brought new life into it. He moved the committee into detailed studies in areas of banking, the Federal Reserve System, and housing. Henry B. was assigned to subcommittees on bank supervision and insurance, consumer affairs, and housing.

In the 88th Congress, fourteen bills of major importance that were handled by the committee became law. Two laws of particular interest to Henry B. were the Urban Mass Transportation Act and the Housing Act of 1964. He played a key role in the passage of the Housing Act, which was considered one of the most important legislative proposals of the New Frontier and Great Society programs. His role was recognized by President Johnson when he was asked to witness the president signing the act into law.

## Face-to-Face Battles

Henry B. never backed down from a face-to-face battle. In 1963, Republican Ed Foreman of Odessa, Texas, questioned Henry B.'s patriotism and called him a "pinko," meaning a communist.[15] Henry B. questioned Foreman during a session of the House. When Foreman answered sarcastically, Henry B. invited him outside to discuss it. Henry B. gave Foreman a tongue lashing and shoved him for emphasis. Foreman went to the news media and accused Henry B. of attacking him. Henry B. denied hitting Foreman and said that Foreman was resorting to irresponsible smear tactics. He added that Foreman's tactics were uncalled-for in the Congress. "I'd still like to have it out with him man for man, but he's a *jate*—that's Spanish for a yellow-livered sissy."[16]

Many newspapers across the country supported Henry B. and criticized Foreman. Foreman stopped questioning the patriotism of Henry B. and others in Congress. When Foreman ran for reelection, Henry B. went to West Texas to help Democrat Dick White unseat him. "The best time to kill a rattler is when he begins to wiggle," Henry B. said.[17]

Henry B. was offered a position on the board of directors of a San Antonio national bank, along with $14,000 in bank stock, because having him on the board would be valuable publicity for to the bank. Henry B. promptly invited the banker who made the offer to leave his office. The situation was made public by Representative Patman in a speech critical of the national banking lobby. Newspapers across the country praised Henry B.'s honesty.

He questioned Federal Aviation Administrator Najeeb Halaby's decision to move the air route traffic control center from San Antonio to New Orleans in 1961. He said Halaby mistook himself "for the king of the people, instead of their servant."[18] Halaby referred to Henry B. as "a freshman congressman acting like a freshman." Henry B. said he would remain "a freshman all of my life if Halaby is an example of a sophomore."[19] In San Antonio he criticized Halaby for his arrogance and rudeness and raised questions about the move itself. He protested to President Kennedy, who had appointed Halaby. He took the fight all the way to congressional leaders. In 1965 President Johnson appointed a new FAA administrator.

Nothing was too big for Henry B. to tackle. He launched a full-scale attack on CBS after its national show *Hunger in America* in the late 1960s. The so-called documentary depicted an infant in a San Antonio hospital supposedly dying of malnutrition. Congressional investigators and the U.S. House Agriculture Appropriations Committee found the claim was false. They also found that other things in the film were false and misleading, not only in San Antonio but nationally.

## A Sad Day for Texans

Texas became the focus of the news worldwide when President Kennedy was assassinated in Dallas on November 22, 1963. The Kennedys, Vice President and Mrs. Johnson, and Governor and Mrs. Connally were making appearances in five Texas cities in two days. The Democrats were fighting in Texas, and the trip was planned to try to smooth over the feud.[20] All of the Texas delegation of representatives were invited to fly in the presidential plane and accompany the president.

Henry B. was one of the delegation and a member of the motorcade. He rode in the parade and introduced President Kennedy when he dedicated the School of Aerospace Medicine at Brooks Air Force Base. San Antonians lined the streets and cheered the motorcade. First Lady Jacqueline Kennedy addressed a crowd in Spanish. There was a warm and enthusiastic welcome for the group.

From San Antonio, the group went to Dallas. Stanley Marcus, founder of Neiman-Marcus and a staunch Democratic supporter, had discouraged the group from appearing in Dallas. There was a sense of general unease. Dallas was an angry town. Marcus told Vice President Johnson, "Lyndon, don't come. You know what it was like when you and Lady Bird were here, you were spit on and hit with picket signs. Don't bring Kennedy to Dallas," he insisted.[21] No one listened to him, because they didn't believe anything would happen to the president.

Henry B. went with the group to Dallas. He was in the fifth car behind President Kennedy in the motorcade. The crowds in Dallas were not as warm and welcoming as those in San Antonio. There were anti-Kennedy signs along the route. "Goldwater for President" signs and bumper stickers were everywhere. A group of Kennedy haters had taken out a full-page ad in the *Dallas Morning News,* and many of the crowd held up the paper for the people in the motorcade to see. When the fatal shot was fired, the cars in the motorcade followed the presidential car to the hospital. After the president was pronounced dead, Henry B. watched as the First Lady took off her wedding ring, placed it on her husband's lifeless finger, and kissed him on the lips. "I just couldn't take it," Henry B. said. "I just choked up completely." He walked away crying.[22] Henry B. and several aides carried President Kennedy's coffin from the hospital to a waiting hearse.

The same San Antonians who had greeted President Kennedy with warmth and love mourned his death with equal depth. The San Fernando Cathedral bells had tolled for many in the past. The dirge bell began its mournful ring at the announcement of President Kennedy's death. Henry B. expressed his grief and anger at the useless death. "Those of us who have been exposed to character assassins have been well aware for many years that there is just a matter of degree between character assassins and real assassins," he said.[23]

---

"They [Chicano militants in La Raza Unida political party] hate me, and the feeling is mutual. If they were my friends, I'd shoot myself."

—Henry B. Gonzalez

*Henry B. Gonzalez, circa 1928, at about twelve years old. He is on the porch of his home at 217 Upson Street.* (Courtesy Gail Beagle)

YOU KNOW MY RECORD

**Henry B. Gonzalez**
**State Senator**
**You Make The Decision**

*Henry B. Gonzalez, campaign poster, 1960.* (Courtesy Gail Beagle)

Congressman
Henry B. Gonzalez,
first Mexican
American elected
to the U.S. House
of Representatives,
circa 1961.
(Courtesy
Gail Beagle)

Luz (Gonzalez) Tamez, director of Henry B.'s San Antonio office; Cora Faye (Dixon) Clayton, personal secretary and constituent casework assistant; and Gail Beagle, chief of staff and press secretary, in 1962. (Courtesy Gail Beagle)

*Henry B. escorting President John F. Kennedy and First Lady Jacqueline Kennedy in San Antonio on November 22, 1964, the day of JFK's assassination.* (Courtesy Gail Beagle)

*Henry B. attended a Farmworker's Union meeting in summer 1964 with daughter Anna (lower left corner with hand on his knee).* (Courtesy Gail Beagle)

*Henry B.'s parents, Leonides and Genoveva Gonzalez, November 14, 1965, at the fifth anniversary of Henry B.'s election to Congress.* (Courtesy Gail Beagle)

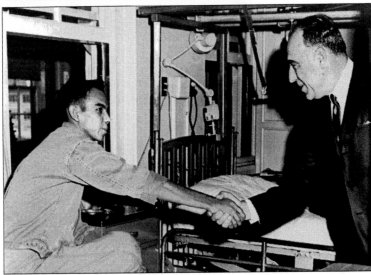

*Henry B. visits wounded soldier at Fort Sam Hospital in 1968.* (Courtesy Gail Beagle)

*Henry B. often posed on Capitol steps with constituents and friends. Photo includes Vicki, Gail, Terri, Larice, and Leroy Beagle, all Texans, in the late 1970s.* (Courtesy Gail Beagle)

*Henry B. and "Chick" Kazen of Laredo in 1983. They have the record for the longest filibuster in Texas history.* (Courtesy Gail Beagle)

*Henry B. was the "sometimes" pitcher for the Democratic-Republican baseball game.* (Courtesy Gail Beagle)

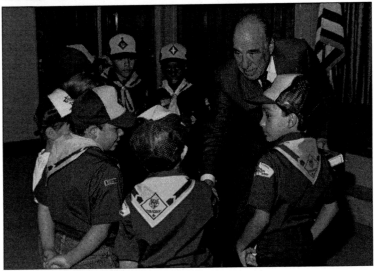

*Henry B. with a group of Cub Scouts in in his 20th Congressional District, January 29, 1988.* (Courtesy Gail Beagle)

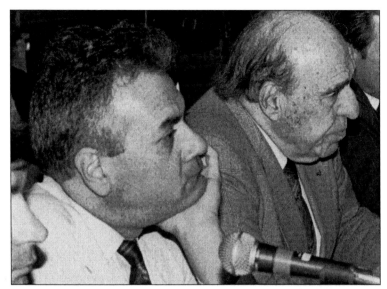

*Henry B. and Congressman Barney Frank, Democrat, Massachusetts, at Banking Committee hearing in 1989.* (Courtesy Gail Beagle)

*Henry B. Gonzalez, chairman of Banking and Housing Committee, 1989.* (Courtesy Gail Beagle)

*Henry B. and Bertha Gonzalez at their golden anniversary party, November 1990.* (Courtesy Rose Mary Gonzalez Ramos)

*The Gonzalez family. From top, left to right: Bertha, Steven, Bertha and Henry B., Genevieve, Charlie, Rose Mary, Frank, and Anna. Henry B. Jr. is missing.* (Courtesy Rose Mary Gonzalez Ramos)

# CHAPTER 10

# *Don Quixote*

Henry B. campaigned for Lyndon B. Johnson in the 1964 presidential election. When Johnson was elected, he supported Johnson's Great Society programs. He disagreed with President Johnson on the United States' involvement in the Vietnam War, but he supported the troops who were there.

On Christmas Eve, 1966, Henry B. met President and Mrs. Johnson when they landed at Kelly Air Force Base in San Antonio. They had come to meet an ambulance plane carrying wounded soldiers. President Johnson went inside the aircraft to greet each man personally. After he had spoken to each soldier, President and Mrs. Johnson, their daughter Lynda, and Henry B. stood at the steps of the plane to greet each young man as he was carried from the aircraft.

The first soldier was lifted from the plane and slowly brought down the steps on a stretcher. A woman rushed past the waiting group, pushing President Johnson aside. She kissed the young man on the stretcher and then said to President Johnson, "I am sorry, Mr. President, but this is my boy. We just heard last night that he had been hit."[1]

Any constituent with a son or daughter in Vietnam could get help from Henry B. Lt. Charlie Jones of the West Side in San Antonio was in Vietnam in 1972. He was on a scouting expedition with a group of infantry when he received a call that he was to report to a brigadier general. Jones was scared and did the thing he had been taught not to do. Upon seeing the general, he saluted. In the battlefield, officers were never saluted, because it could get them killed or taken as prisoner of war. Jones was so nervous he forgot the rule.

The general, who had been brought back from Hawaii, where he had gone for a rest from the war, was not happy with Jones. He did not waste words in letting Jones know that he should not have saluted him. Then he asked him if he knew why he was there. Jones didn't know. The general said to a sergeant, "Give the lieutenant a pencil and paper." When Jones had the paper in hand, the general said, "Write your mother!"[2] Charlie Jones' mother was a constituent of Congressman Henry B. Gonzalez. When she did not hear from her son, she went to the Red Cross for help. The Red Cross could not find him. She went to Henry B. for help. Henry B. found Charlie Jones, and Jones wrote to his mother!

Henry B. followed some advice about pleasing constituents that Lyndon Johnson had shared with him: he built card files in which to keep track of his contacts with constituents. He stapled notes on them about each letter written. He knew no color barrier in dealing with his constituents. He treated all with equal respect and concern for their problems. "Henry, regardless of his immense duties as chair of the Banking Committee, has never overlooked his constituents," said Ruben Escobedo, a constituent.[3] He not only took care of his constituents but anyone who asked him for help. He always carried a note pad with him to write down questions and requests. He never forgot to respond, especially to students and the elderly. He had an open-door policy at his Washington office as well as in San Antonio.

## Loyal Office Staff

There was not much turnover in staff in either the Washington or the San Antonio office. Henry B. "just assumed that if you worked for him, you had the same philosophical beliefs," said Mary Jessie Roque, who worked in the San Antonio office for over thirty years. "It was exciting to work for him. He spoke his mind, and you never knew what he was going to say."[4] His staff in both offices teasingly referred to him as "Don Quixote." The staff in the Washington office dealt primarily with legislative issues. The San Antonio office dealt mostly in casework. "A lot of people contacted Congressman Gonzalez because they didn't know where else to go," said Roque.[5]

Someone on the staff interviewed anyone who came to the offices. The visitor was then referred to the proper federal agency or scheduled an appointment with Henry B. He referred those from other districts to their own representatives as a matter of congressional courtesy. If the person could not get help from his own congressman, Henry B. tried to help regardless of district. When he was in Washington, he called his San Antonio office every morning and had someone read all the articles in the local paper that referred to him or any issues of interest to him. "He had an incredible mind," said Roque. "He not only could remember what was written, he remembered who wrote it and when."[6]

He responded to all veterans whether they were in his district or not. He worked for veterans' rights to health care, better pay, and benefits that had been promised when they enlisted in the service. Delores Gamez of San Antonio appealed to Henry B. for help in burial expenses for her father. Although her father was a Navy veteran of World War II and the Korean War, the Veterans Affairs office rejected her request. They said they had no record of her father's service. She wrote to Henry B. explaining all the details of the request and rejection. Henry B. intervened for her. The VA office promptly wrote her a letter of apology and sent a check to reimburse her for the expenses.[7]

## Long-Distance Family Man

By the time Henry B. went to Washington, he and Bertha had eight children. He once remarked that after he went to Washington, that took care of having children. In Bertha's witty way, she said, "If that could have been done by remote control, we would have had another one."[8] Henry B. couldn't afford to move the family to Washington, because living expenses were too high, but he flew home almost every weekend. He also stayed in touch daily. The whole family visited him in Washington each summer. His oldest grandson, Henry B. Gonzalez III, often spent summers with his grandfather and traveled with him when he made speeches.

Henry B. flew home from Washington almost every weekend, and Sunday was family time. One of the family activities in San Antonio was to stuff and sort envelopes on

Sunday afternoons. It was a family tradition that everyone ate Sunday lunch together. Before the children could do anything else, they had to form an assembly line and help Henry B. with his mail. Henry B. insisted that he sign every piece of mail that went out of his offices. Unlike other members of congress who had auto-pens, he never used one. He either dictated letters or his staff wrote correspondence to reflect his ideas. Then he read the letters, corrected or approved them, and sent them back for final typing. On Sunday afternoons, all of his correspondence from his two offices was put on the dining table. Henry B. signed the letters before the children folded them and stuffed the envelopes. Then all of the stamped envelopes were sorted for mailing. The children knew there was no playing outside until the work was done.

Although his time was limited, Henry B. was a family man. He taught each one of his children how to swim. He camped and hiked with them. He was involved with community activities. Occasionally there was time to go to the park and throw the football for the boys. "That is the greatest memory I have. It's not this big spectacular family vacation and it's not about Disneyland. The neat experiences are the down times, the throwing of the football, watching you, helping you with a lesson," said Charlie.[10] The extended family of "aunts, uncles, grandparents on both sides had a great influence on us as children," Henry B. Jr. said. "Dad sacrificed quantity time by being in politics, but we had quality time that made up the difference."[11]

Henry B. tried to set an example for his children to follow. He often gave them tidbits of advice. "Start something, finish it." "Whatever you produce, the end results reflect on

85

you." "Do unto others as you would have them do unto you." "A closed mouth, a fly will never enter."

"Dad set a good example," said Henry B. Jr. "He made an effort to give his best on any project he started."[12] Besides giving advice, he set an example by his own love of reading. He showed his children the importance of a good education.

## Great Believer in Education

"Congressman Gonzalez was a great believer in the importance and the power of education," said Tod Wells, who worked on Henry B.'s legislative staff in Washington for eight years. "He often stayed in his office until late at night to read books, magazines, and newspapers about current events, philosophy, economics, and even mathematics. All the things he read were at some time reflected in the speeches he gave on the floor of the House of Representatives."[13] "Dad set an example for us kids because we saw him reading all the time and he used what he read in discussions. But as far as Dad monitoring our school progress, he left it to Mom," Charlie said. "He was unable to do a lot of things, because he chose a career that kept him away from the house. However, his influence was still felt by us."[14]

"Dad worried about his own children's education," said Henry B. Jr. "He believed in public schools, but he wanted his children to have religious training, so we went to private Catholic schools."[15] They lived in a small parish that did not offer the religious training that Henry B. felt was important in first through seventh grades. Also, public schools were segregated and private schools were not. The children had grown up in a neighborhood with different ethnic groups. Henry B. and Bertha wanted their children to see individuals, not the color of their skins.

The family who lived across the alley from them on Morton Street was African American. The neighborhood children played together in an interracial group, although some of Henry B. Jr.'s friends were not allowed to play with African Americans. Henry B. talked to his children about segregation being an injustice to humanity. They were always aware that their father was involved with civil rights movements for Mexican Americans and African Americans. The Gonzalez children walked past two elementary schools on their way to the parochial school. Kinley Elementary was for Anglo children, and two blocks away was Gonzalez Elementary for minorities, primarily Mexican Americans. "Dad was disappointed when his grandchildren went to parochial schools," said Henry B. Jr. "He just believed so strongly in the power of public education."[16]

## Great Respect for Teachers and Students

Henry B. had great respect for teachers, and he never forgot his own teachers. He sent Gladys Stallings, his English teacher at Mark Twain Middle School, a Christmas card every year. "She always said that he was an excellent student who took school seriously," said Stallings' daughter, Carlita Kosty.[17] He also sent Stallings and other teachers magazines and print material from Washington that he thought could be used in the classroom. Kosty followed in her mother's footsteps and became a teacher. In the late 1980s she arranged for five Sam Rayburn Middle School eighth graders to interview Henry B. for a history project in her class. The interview was on a Saturday right after Christmas, and they met him in his office. "He spent over four hours patiently answering questions and acted like that was the most important thing on his mind. He made the students feel very special," Kosty said.[18]

Eiginio Rodriguez was in elementary school in the 1970s when he met Henry B. The U.S. flag at his school was in tatters. His teacher told him that he would have to write Congress for a replacement. Henry B. personally delivered a new flag to the school. He spoke with Rodriguez and his brother as friends. He reminded all of the children of the importance of education and quoted John F. Kennedy's words, "Ask not what your country can do for you, ask what you can do for your country."[19]

"He never turned down an invitation to visit schools and had picture after picture made with the students," said Lucille Santos, longtime San Antonio educator. "He always had time to talk to the students. And he always had time to address educational needs. When a school did not have a flag, he brought one that had flown over the Capitol and gave it to the students. When there were no funds for programs, he always tried to find the money for those most needy."[20] Dressed in his white suit and white shoes, Henry B. was a favorite with students and teachers.

## A Loner in Washington

Henry B. wasn't a part of the social circuit in Washington. He often read late into the night in his office. He personally read each letter that was sent to him from constituents, from people around the country who saw him on C-Span, or from people around the world who learned of his efforts in the U.S. Congress.[21] He lived in a small efficiency apartment on the House side of the Capitol. It was very close to his work. For many years he didn't have a car in Washington. Once he had a car, he drove to events in Virginia or Maryland, to Farhney's, his favorite pen shop, and to Trover Bookstore on Pennsylvania Avenue. When he had time, he browsed through used bookstores. He was usually the pitcher in the annual baseball game between the Democrats and Republicans. When the game was moved from Washington to Boston, he didn't join the team. "I didn't mind making a fool of myself, but I'm not going to drive forty miles to do it," he explained.[22]

Social invitations in Washington came primarily from constituents who were in Washington for legislative conferences. There were Capitol Hill receptions where constituents met with their congressman. He hosted people for lunches or breakfasts in the House Restaurant at the Capitol. He received some White House invitations that came primarily through Democrats. He attended events and dinners both in Washington and in San Antonio where he was the main speaker.

Occasionally, he went to someone's home. His friends from Laredo, Oscar and Elsa Laurel, lived in Washington while Oscar Laurel was on the National Transportation Board. He and Henry B. had served together in the Texas legislature. The Laurels sometimes invited Henry B. and his staff to their home for dinner. One time he and his staff were invited to dine at the home of Ernie, the maitre d' of the House Restaurant. Ernie was an African American from Jamaica and spoke fluent Spanish. He entertained the group for hours telling about his experiences—both good and bad—working for and with legislators. Often he was treated as if he were invisible. Some of the congressmen even made racial slurs within his hearing. He mimicked the congressmen, which was made funnier by his Jamaican accent.[23]

In the early years of Henry B.'s career, there was a lot of prejudice in Washington, directed primarily at African Americans and women. African Americans were not allowed to eat in the House Restaurant with the other congressmen. Adam Clayton Powell, a tall, slender, light-skinned, and handsome black man, was assigned a small room where he was served separately. In the early 1960s, a congressman from San Angelo and later part of San Antonio wrote a scathing newspaper article denouncing Washington as the "Nigger capitol."[24] Henry B. knew about prejudice and how to deal with it. He hired Cora Faye Dixon, the first African American secretary in Congress. No one could complain about Dixon, a graduate of Our Lady of the Lake University in San Antonio, because she was an excellent secretary and an asset to his office. She worked for him for thirty years as a constituent caseworker as well as secretary.

Women were mistreated more subtly than African Americans, but they still suffered discrimination. The Democratic Staff Members Club sent out notices of suppers in the House Cafeteria. Gail Beagle and an associate decided to attend one night. They were the only women there. Although they stayed through the meal, it was made clear that it was for men only. There was a group called the Texas Breakfast Club that met on the Hill. The members were all staff employees who were originally from Texas. The notices were circulated among the offices. It was not stated that the gatherings were for men only, but it was understood. Gail Beagle attended one morning and realized that she was the only women there. A male friend said, "Don't leave."[25] She stayed and eventually joined the group. There were many state societies in Washington organized by the people from various states. The societies, an elitist group of professional and intellectual members, were for white men only. It wasn't until the 1970s that drastic changes took place and both minorities and women were included in the groups.

Henry B. fought prejudice and segregation where he found it. And he had found it in the U.S. House of Representatives.

---

"Dad was on a mission. He never forgot a person nor an issue. He had an incredible memory," said Charlie.[26] "He opened eyes, he opened hearts, and that shall be my father's legacy."[27]

# CHAPTER 11

# *The Eccentric*

Not everyone loved Henry B. or agreed with him. His opponents called him "eccentric" and accused him of "tilting windmills," or fighting imaginary problems. "Organized crime has penetrated the highest level of our government. They're *in* there," Henry B. warned the public in the late 1970s.[1] He blamed Attorney General John Mitchell during the Nixon Administration. "King Crime, as I call it, has literally taken over the country ... It has penetrated business all the way from banks to shopping centers to savings and loans and to insurance companies. It has certainly penetrated the highest levels of the federal government for years," declared Henry B.[2]

In the 1976 presidential campaign, a number of Democratic delegates considered Henry B. seriously for Jimmy Carter's running mate. Henry B. was not interested. He further alienated himself from the group a year later when he resigned as chairman of the House Committee on Assassinations. He said, "I've had it with that miserable clot of yo-yos."[3] Henry B. suspected a conspiracy surrounding Kennedy's death. Although investigations went on for years, a conspiracy was never proven.

## The Visionary

Henry B. was not only an antagonist in issues, he was a visionary. He discovered that the Atomic Energy Commission had known about the dangers of nuclear power and had kept the knowledge from the American people and Congress. He studied all of the House and Senate debates on licensing private nuclear power in 1954. "Unbelievable," he reported to Congress. "Not in all of that voluminous number of turgid pages of prose was there even one word with reference to safety or to the undesirable products resulting from that kind of activity. Not one word. It is just absolutely incredible. The people have been lied to. The Congress has been kept in blinders."[4] He introduced a bill in Congress to prohibit any more building of nuclear fission power plants. The bill called for the gradual stop of plants in operation. It also called on President Carter to order the U.S. ambassador to the United Nations to reverse the American example to the world on nuclear power. None of the bills passed Congress.

He was a visionary in the use of solar power. About San Antonio Henry B. said, "With our abundant sunlight and the very substantial amount of solar experience, no place in the country is better suited than San Antonio to develop solar power on a large-scale basis."[5] He said that the city should adopt building-code provisions to encourage the installation of solar units in new homes. He proposed that City Public Service help to pay for the units. He also suggested that the city could study using solar power in its own buildings to "provide a useful example for everyone."[6] Again, no one listened.

Nationally, along with several colleagues, he wrote a let-

93

ter calling for a visionary commitment to solar energy as the U.S. preferred energy source. The letter argued that solar power would reduce subsidies to competing fuels. Health care costs would be lower, as unhealthful energy sources would be reduced. Pollution and waste costs would be reduced. None of Henry B.'s visionary suggestions were taken seriously nor acted upon by the president or Congress. He disagreed that raising consumer prices would control the energy problems. No one stopped driving when lines formed at the gas pumps and prices almost doubled. By the end of his lifetime, there was an energy crisis. Utility bills had skyrocketed because of the price of coal, gas, and oil. There was an alarming amount of pollution in the air and water. The state and federal governments subsidized gas and oil companies.

"The Democrats are acting like Republicans," Henry B. said, "and they'll be a minority party if they keep it up."[7] Again, he was right. President Carter was in trouble for re-election in 1980. Many Democrats were what Henry B. called "barking-dog politicians—you throw a little bone and they shut up."[8] He opposed President Carter's oil-price decontrol program. "There has to be some kind of balance between the interests of consumers and producers," he explained.[9] When the Democrats joined the Republicans in proposing ways to balance the U.S. budget, Henry B. said, "The American people are being crucified on a cross of the balanced budget."[10] Americans were so unhappy with Carter's administration that they elected a former movie star and governor of California, Republican Ronald Reagan, as president.

## Gone Too Far?

Many of Henry B.'s colleagues thought he had gone too

far in the 1980s when he called for the impeachment of former Federal Reserve Board Chairman Arthur Burns. But criticism didn't stop him from calling things the way he saw them. In 1981 Henry B. introduced a resolution to impeach Federal Reserve Chairman Paul A. Volcker for pushing up interest rates. Former energy secretary Bill Richardson, who had served with Henry B., noted in hindsight that a review of the economy, the savings and loan crisis, and the recession under Burns' term of office called for a different conclusion. "You know, Henry B. was right. We should have impeached the guy," Richardson said.[11]

In 1982, Henry B. called Samuel R. Pierce Jr., the secretary of Housing and Urban Development and then the only black member of the Reagan cabinet, a "Stepin Fetchit," referring to a black comedian whose trademark was a slow shuffle and an exaggerated southern drawl. He believed that Pierce was more interested in pleasing the administration than he was in helping poor people. He thought that Pierce talked down to others of his race as if they were inferior to him. He also thought that Pierce lacked pride in his own heritage. Henry B. would not back down, although he was heavily criticized for the statement.

## Another Battle of Name-Calling

In 1986 Henry B. and an aide were eating breakfast at Earl Abel's restaurant in San Antonio. His aide told Henry B. that he had overheard a man at a nearby table call Henry B. a communist. Seventy-year-old Henry B. confronted the man, Bill Allen. He asked Allen if he had called him a communist. Allen admitted that he had. According to newspaper reports, Henry B. punched Allen. Henry B. said that although he had been provoked, he acted in a restrained manner. "If I had acted out of passion, that fellow would still not be able to eat *chalupas*," he said.[12] Henry B. Jr., an attorney, advised his dad, "Just lay low for a while and it will blow over."[13] Allen filed assault charges against Henry B. but later dropped the charges. He told reporters that he had overheard Henry B. criticizing President Reagan. As in the Foreman case in 1963, the press took Henry B.'s side.

## The Constitutionist

Henry B. was a constitutionist and believed that the Executive Branch of government and Congress should go by the book. Republicans and Democrats refused to support him when he called for the impeachment of President Ronald Reagan for violating the War Powers Act after the United States invasion of Grenada in October 1983. He was criticized by his colleagues and the press. He ignored the criticisim.

In 1987 he introduced a resolution to impeach President Reagan over the United States' involvement in selling illegal arms to Iran. President Reagan denied knowing about the diversion of funds to the Contras, although others testified that he had approved the actions. Many documents were destroyed, and some federal employees lost their jobs. But few supported Henry B.'s call for impeachment of the president. Henry B. believed that in both cases, the constitution had been violated. President Reagan had made decisions without the required consent of the Congress. "The Reagan administration broke nearly every national and international law on the books," he said.[14] "Here you had a president who felt that just because he didn't like the leader of some other nation, he could use the military might of the air to topple him without getting congressional permission."[15]

## Chairman of the House Banking Committee

Henry B. became a national figure in legislation when he became the chairman of the House Banking Committee in the House of Representatives. He had warned of a crisis in the savings and loan industry in 1988. No one wanted a scandal in a presidential election year, so he was ignored. When former House Banking Committee chairman Fernand St. Germain, a Democrat from Rhode Island, lost his reelection bid, many Capitol Hill insiders were alarmed. Henry B. had seniority and was next in line in the House of Representatives for the chairmanship.

"He is definitely a little quirky," said Representative Barney Frank, a Massachusetts Democrat who had worked closely with Henry B. on housing matters. "He is not the most conventional person. He says what he wants to say and wears what he wants to wear. But he is very well informed, and, believe it or not, a very kind person. I think he will be a good chairman."[16] Henry B. did cut a striking figure in his electric blue two-piece suit and white silk tie, or his Kelly green sport jacket with yellow or wildly printed ties. (Although some reported the suits to be off-the-rack polyester, they were, in fact, fashioned by a San Antonio tailor.) The "mad Mexican" was actually among the more intellectually cultivated in Congress.[17] He just didn't always dress as conservatively as the rest of the members.

When Henry B. took over the leadership of the Banking Committee in 1989, he was the most powerful

Mexican American in Congress, and he had a reputation of being outside the mainstream. He made a lot of powerful financial interests in the country nervous because he was not part of the Washington "ol' boy network"—he never had been and didn't ever want to be. His leadership as chairman was challenged twice. He didn't act like the majority. He didn't dress like the majority. He didn't talk like Washington dealmakers. And he didn't compromise on issues of major importance.

## A Contrast in Styles

Henry B. stood out in contrast to the Senate Banking chairman, Donald W. Riegle Jr. Riegle was very quiet and cautious in making any remarks about his position and what he hoped to accomplish. Henry B. was open to questions from anyone. Riegle believed that President Bush should take the lead to solve the banking problems. Henry B. and his committee solved the problems and Bush supported them.

Henry B. won over some of his critics soon after becoming chairman. "Bankers and the Fed have feared him, but most real bankers like what he's done," said John White, a former Texas agriculture commissioner.[18] "One thing bankers like is how Gonzalez gives them the floor," said U.S. Representative Steve Bartlett, Republican committee member from Dallas. "Put simply, he lets people talk." Bartlett added, "Mr. Gonzalez and I fight like rattlesnakes and roadrunners; we're poles apart philosophically, particularly on public housing issues, but had he been committee chairman four years earlier, when savings and loan legislation was called for, we would not be in the mess we're in now."[19]

"If there were such a thing as chairman-of-the-year award, Henry would be the uncontested winner," said Iowa's Representative Jim Leach, the committee's second-ranking Republican. "He's brought an even-handed approach to our work. His position is now unchallenged."[20] In response to the praise for Henry B., Bertha Gonzalez said, "I still think Henry works too hard sometimes, but I have never thought it wasn't worth it. It's time he did get recognition for trying to get the crooks out of the way. But no matter what happens, I don't think he'll change."[21]

## Another Money Scandal

By the time President Bush signed the savings and loan bailout legislation, Henry B.'s performance had impressed even his critics. The legislation saved senior citizens and poor people from losing their life savings. When that job was done, Henry B. pushed for an investigation of the Lincoln Savings and Loan scandal. The investigation embarrassed five U.S. senators, including four Democrats, and forced the Office of Thrift Supervision chief, Danny Wall, to resign. Many Democrats would have avoided the Lincoln S&L probe because it exposed the dishonesty of powerful senators in their own party. Henry B.'s actions shocked many cynical Washington observers. The Republicans acknowledged grudgingly that he was fair when working in the legislative process.

Democratic U.S. Representative Joe Kennedy said, "When I came to Washington, I was delighted to serve on the Banking Committee because I knew there was one individual who I could always turn to on that committee to learn how the poor were going to be affected by a particu-

lar vote, to cut through all the baloney and the highfalutin'
talk we hear in Washington. Henry B. Gonzalez sits up
there as chairman and cuts through all the baloney."[22]

## Out of the Center

Everyone knew that Henry B. couldn't be bought, and
time after time, he proved that he would not back down because of criticism. When President George Bush launched
Operation Desert Storm in the Persian Gulf War in 1991,
Henry B. called for the impeachment of the president for
sending troops to war without the vote of Congress. Henry
B.'s resolution to impeach was very unpopular among both
Democrats and Republicans and caused him to receive
death threats. He refused to back down. He said his impeachment resolutions were based on the constitutional
right of Congress, not the executive branch, to declare war.

He infuriated the Republicans who called for a repri-
mand of Henry B. and forced a vote for the Ethics
Committee to review Henry B.'s behavior. The vote failed.
He said, "I can't say how pleased I am that the Republicans
listen and read my Special Orders. It must have hit pretty
close to those goose-steppers."[23] Editorials in newspapers
countrywide, including in his own hometown, criticized
him, and some called him names. A reporter asked him
about being called "eccentric" and explained the word
came from the Latin *ex centro,* which means "out of the center." Henry B. thought about it and said, "Out of the center . . . I can live with that."[24]

100

"He was independent. He did not care about the hot shots or the big timers who came in . . . trying to tell people what to do. He ignored all of that. He did exactly what he wanted to do."
—U.S. Representative Maxine Waters,
Democrat from California

# CHAPTER 12

## *Honest Henry*

Henry B.'s health began declining in July 1997, when he had to be taken by ambulance from the House floor. He had a severe dental infection that had damaged a heart valve and threatened his life. After surgery, his cardiologist ordered him to remain home and to avoid crowds. His resistance was low, and a contagious infection could lodge in the weakened heart valve. He announced that he would resign from the House of Representatives at the end of the year. But then he changed his mind.

Henry B. was determined to go back to Washington. He worked with weights and took walks to rebuild his strength, but he continued to lose weight. Each day he called his offices in Washington and San Antonio. He signed all official correspondence brought to his house by aides. After fourteen months of being away from Washington, Henry B. returned to the Capitol on September 24, 1998, to vote on several bills. He pronounced himself ready to "register the voice of the vote."[1]

Although frail from his illness, he responded to everyone who spoke to him on the trip to Washington. Sitting in the Dallas airport, he was approached by a blind man who was selling something. Without looking at what it was, Henry B. took two dollars from his pocket and bought the item—a tiny set of screwdrivers, the kind used to repair eyeglasses. "It's always been hard from me to say no, even when I didn't have anything," Henry B. said of the exchange. "It reminds me of something I once heard: Charity isn't giving a dog a bone; it's giving a dog a bone when you're just as hungry."[2] No one was expecting to see "the dean of the Texas congressional delegation"[3] in Washington. Both Democrats and Republicans welcomed him back with praises.

## Praises End

Henry B. was a shell of the robust man he had been. He was thin and pale. His critics began to call on him to resign and forfeit his $136,000 yearly salary. After serving his constituents for thirty-seven years, he refused to resign from Congress. House Speaker Newt Gingrich and House Majority Leader Dick Armey, both Republicans, stayed silent about the popular Democrat's absence. Democratic House Minority Leader Dick Gephardt said, "Congressman Gonzalez's constituents are getting full services from his office. He is keeping track of it."[4] Some San Antonio critics said he was trying to hold the position to help his son, former state district judge Charlie Gonzalez, who had announced his candidacy for District 20.

Had Henry B. resigned, Governor George W. Bush would have had to call for a special election. Henry B. said he had saved the taxpayers more than $300,000, the cost of a special election. "Even though I may have missed, I will find a way to be there to register my vote on any critical occasion, and it may be that we are approaching that now with respect to the president," Henry B. said in August 1998.[5]

## No Apologies Made

Henry B. made his last trip to Washington, D.C., on December 19, 1998, to vote against the impeachment of President Bill Clinton. President Clinton, a Democrat, was accused of lying under oath about his affair with a White House intern, Monica Lewinsky. His presidency had been plagued with investigations and hearings about his private life. In defending his support of the president, Henry B. said, "This is a personal flaw and a failure on the part of the president. It's of a moral nature, not political."[6]

His critics reminded him that he had called for the impeachment of the two former Republican presidents. He made no apology for having called for the impeachment of Ronald Reagan and George Bush. He said he took those measures when when both presidents sent U.S. military troops to other countries without the consent of Congress. He considered the actions a violation of the nation's laws. He reminded them that he was just as critical of President Clinton and his administration for bombing two terrorist camps in Afghanistan and Sudan without support and aid from allied nations.

## Humble Henry B. Steps Down

In November 1998, after Henry B. had announced that he was not going to run for another term in office, an editorial in the *San Antonio Express-News* praised him for his thirty-seven years of service. "From the assassination of his friend John Kennedy, to the fall of Newt Gingrich, Gonzales was an eye-witness to history—and singularly bipartisan about sounding off against injustice."[7] Henry B. officially stepped down from his House seat on December 31, 1998. He was replaced in the November election by his son Charlie. Congressman Charlie Gonzalez was sworn in as the representative of the 20th District of Texas in January 1999.

After serving nineteen terms in the House, a humble Henry B. said, "When you consider the total number of people who have served in Congress, it's very small. It really is a tremendous honor. I don't guess you could have a higher honor, because it's a solid expression of confidence from your neighbors and citizens. What more could you ask for?"[8]

## Against All Odds

Against all odds, Henry B. lost his first run for an elective office by only 100 votes. Years later, Bertha teased him that it was a shame he hadn't been "whipped real good, so you wouldn't still be fooling around with politics."[9] Henry B. ran for public office when he was warned that no one would vote for a "Mexican." He became the first Mexican American to serve on San Antonio City Council, to be elected to the Texas Senate, and to be elected to the U.S. House of Representatives. He went against his own party to defeat proposed segregation legislation and to change existing segregation laws.

Henry B. was urged to run for the vice presidency in 1968 and 1972. There were bumper sticker campaigns in both Texas and Arizona. "I wouldn't have it on a bet," he told a reporter. "Legislative advocacy is my field. I'm trained for it, and happy in it. It is the height of honor."[10] In 1989, Sam Rayburn Middle School eighth graders asked him if he would ever run for president. He told them, "I have had never had a desire to become president. I love the legislative part of the government and prefer working directly with the people."[11]

Henry B. was well known in the House for his "special orders" speeches. The special orders was a block of time televised by C-Span in which House members could take the floor and speak on any subject. Henry B. used the time more than anyone else. He exposed what he thought were injustices to the American people. He criticized both Democrats and Republicans for their shortsightedness regarding the financial well-being of the country. He warned of an energy crisis. He called for the impeachment of government officials whom he believed were not following constitutional law. "His own fluent vocabulary and impeccable command of the grammatical usage set a powerful example. I've heard him speak extemporaneously for an hour in after-session 'special orders' on the House floor. The transcripts read like Emerson's essays," said Jim Wright, a former speaker of the U.S. House of Representatives.[12]

## Understanding Henry B.

Journalists tried to put Henry B. into a political category, but he didn't fit any mold. He was a loner who based his judgment on the facts as he knew them. He was as critical of the Democratic Party as he was the Republican Party. Journalist Paul Burka wrote: "Henry B. has never gotten the credit he deserves because he has never lived up to his potential in Congress. He is too unbending, too unwilling to play by the insiders' rules to be a success at legislative policies. He has the disease of the fifties' Texas liberal who would rather lose and remain pure than win. . . ."[13]

"His personality was far too prickly to allow him to gain the power in Congress that his seniority should have merited," wrote Rick Casey. "But if his weakness was his readiness to fight, his strength was his willingness to fight."[14]

"The enigma of Henry B. was that after thirty years in Congress he was still unbought, unabused and apparently largely unimpressed with even the leadership of his own political party. He is the ultimate outsider who got inside," said Robert Moreno, a journalist.[15]

"Throughout his career, he has stood alone," said Maria Davis, former economist for the Federal Reserve.[16]

Henry B. was unique because of his "basic belief that the first and foremost thing for an elected official is the relationship to the people in his district and their needs," said Frank DeStefano, a congressional staffer who worked with Henry B. for many years. Henry B. was "one of the few people who [lived] by their beliefs on a daily basis and put them into practice. You couldn't find a person more committed to helping the poor and the working man."[17]

## For the Record

Henry B. gained national recognition when he opposed legislation that led to the savings and loan crisis. As chairman of the House Banking Committee from 1989 to 1994, Henry B. oversaw the passage of three major banking bills that reformed the savings and loan industry, tightened banking regulations, and established interstate branch banking. He won the support of his committee as well as all Americans when he took the side of depositors over bankers and land developers.

He attracted worldwide attention by his filibusters against various bills upholding the principles of segregation. He was the champion of civil rights. He was in the center of the struggle to do away with Jim Crow laws. He introduced a bill to end the poll tax, which kept poor people of all races from voting. He also fought against a state sales tax and increases in tuition at state colleges and universities which affected the poor. Foremost in his mind were the needs of his constituency. He worked for "education; water; more industry for San Antonio; minimum wage; benefits for farm workers, civil service workers, veterans; active armed forces personnel; housing; and equal opportunity regardless of race, color, creed, or sex."[18]

Henry B. counted these things among his greatest accomplishments for San Antonio: bringing Hemisfair 1968 to the city; securing federal grants to build the Medical Center; flood-control investments that include portions of the River Walk and Olmos Dam; building public and low-cost housing; securing a 450-bed Brooke Army Medical Center; and establishing Kelly AFB as one of the largest aircraft-repair depots for the U.S. Air Force.

The racial slurs that once followed Henry B. were replaced with titles such as "father of modern Hispanic politics," "a champion of the poor in America," and "a crusader for civil rights." He earned the respect of his constituents and his colleagues by his treatment of others and by remaining honest to himself. Here are just a few of Henry B.'s many honors:

Shallcross Award—1985

M. Justin Herman Memorial Award—1988

*Shelterforce* gave Henry B. a 100 percent score in a Housing Scorecard, ranking members of Congress based upon their voting records on housing legislation.

National Alliance to End Homelessness Award—1991

National Rural Housing Legislator of the Year—1992

John F. Kennedy Profile in Courage Award—1994

Assistance Council Special Award—1996.


## Time with Bertha

"In any study of what makes Henry run, it would be remiss not to mention one factor that certainly played a part in his jump from the state Senate to Congress. That would be his wife, Bertha, and eight children. Even a magician couldn't feed, clothe, and shelter a family that size on a $4,800-a-year State Senate salary as she did," wrote James McCrory.[19] Maury Maverick agreed. "The best thing Henry ever did was to marry his wife, Bertha, a country girl from Floresville," he said. "She is a high-toned intellectual."[20] "Dad's secret weapon was Mom in the background," said Charlie Gonzalez.[21] She ruled the family with an iron hand. Henry B. and Bertha celebrated their sixtieth wedding anniversary on November 10, 2000.

Henry B. was looking forward to spending more time with Bertha and the grandchildren on the Texas coast after he retired. "I want to go to the coast with the grandchildren, and I have plenty of them," he said with a tired but warm smile. "They keep me alive."[22] He and Bertha decided to sell their large home in Monte Vista and move to a smaller one near the Health Science Center. While Bertha packed, Henry B. read, grumbled about moving, and planned for an office at St. Mary's University. There he would arrange and formalize his legislative papers.

## ¡Viva, Henry B.!

But the plans for the future were not to be. Henry B. was taken to Baptist Medical Center from his Monte Vista home for precautionary tests on the morning of November 28, 2000. He was running a fever, which indicated an infection. He died that afternoon, surrounded by his family. Henry B. and Bertha were to have moved on Thursday, November 30, to their smaller home from their house of thirty-five years.

His funeral was attended by over 1,100 people and televised for all of San Antonio. The "rich, the poor, the powerful, the disadvantaged, the young and old"[23] filled San Fernando Cathedral and spilled over into the street. A mariachi band played "Amigo" as Henry B.'s flag-draped coffin was carried from the church to the hearse by six men standing in the crowd on the street. "Picking people from the crowd is how Henry B. would have wanted it," said Kathleen Dora, who works for Congressman Charlie Gonzalez.[24]

San Fernando Cathedral bells tolled as the funeral procession left for the cemetery. Mourners lined the streets from the cathedral to San Fernando Cemetery No. 2, where Henry B. was buried beside his parents, Leonides and Genoveva Gonzalez. All along the route, people held signs that said, "Thank you, Henry B." "Viva Henry B." "We love you, Henry B." "Rest in peace, Henry B."

## Final Tributes

It was fitting that the U.S. House of Representatives' tribute took place during "special orders" on C-Span. Both Democrats and Republicans described him as "the father of modern Hispanic politics," "a champion of the poor in America," and "a crusader for civil rights." Some laughed about his contrariness in a warm, affectionate way. They praised him for his honesty and openness, referring to him as "Honest Henry."

"In thirty-seven years, he accumulated little more than a modest home, a minor rental property, a bit of stock and a couple of passbook accounts. . . . I fear that America may never again see another member of Congress who supports himself, and a large, beautiful family, solely on a congressional salary," wrote columnist Carlos Guerra.[25]

Henry B. was a unique politician. He accepted no money that implied influence on his votes or a bribe for his support. He said, "I walked through the mud of San Antonio politics. I walked through the mud of state politics in Austin. And for thirty years I've walked through the mud in Washington, D.C., and I still haven't gotten the tips of my shoes dirty."[26]

Henry B.'s family received hundreds of tributes to him, from presidents, congressmen, and constituents, following his death. A tribute written by journalist Cary Clack perhaps summarizes them all:

> His conscience appeared so restless that only death could make it still.
> Money couldn't buy it. Fame couldn't seduce it. Complacency couldn't quell it. Threats couldn't

scare it. Ridicule couldn't shake it. And power couldn't overwhelm it.

He was a profound and prophetic conscience. [27]

---

"Henry B. championed those who were less fortunate. He helped fight for civil rights, affordable housing, and economic justice for all. We will all miss Henry's unique contributions, his leadership, passion and sense of fair play for all."

—Former vice president Al Gore

---

"I am especially grateful for his friendship and steadfast support for me personally, and his strength, and [for] standing for what he believes in no matter how great the opposing forces."

—Former president Bill Clinton

# CHRONOLOGY

| | |
|---|---|
| 1916 | Born in San Antonio, Texas, on May 3. |
| 1937 | Received associate degree from San Antonio Junior College. |
| 1937 | Attended the University of Texas at Austin. |
| 1940 | Married Bertha Cuellar in St. Philip Catholic church on November 23. |
| 1941–44 | Served as civilian cable censor for military intelligence. |
| 1943 | Received law degree form St. Mary's University School of Law. |
| 1946 | Served as Bexar County's chief probation officer. |
| 1950–51 | Served as deputy director of Bexar County Housing Authority. |
| 1953–56 | Served as deputy director of Bexar County Housing Authority. |
| 1956 | First Mexican American elected to the Texas Senate. |
| 1957 | Joined Senator Abraham "Chick" Kazen of Laredo in longest filibuster in Texas history by speaking in the Texas Senate against segregationist legislation. |

| | |
|---|---|
| 1957 | Became the first Mexican American to run for Texas governor. |
| 1960 | Re-elected to the Texas Senate. |
| 1961 | Lost campaign for U.S. Senate. |
| 1961 | Elected on November 4 special election to the U.S. House of Representatives, 20th District; first Mexican American to serve in the U.S. House of Representatives. |
| 1962 | First vote in Congress supported a bill to spend $1.5 billion on construction of academic facilities at public and private colleges. |
| 1963 | Texas Republican Congressman Ed Foreman accused Henry B. of being a communist. |
| 1962 | Rode in President Kennedy's motorcade when Kennedy was assassinated in Dallas on November 22. |
| 1964 | Supported Civil Rights Act, worked on Equal Opportunities Act. |
| 1965 | Landmark Voting Rights Act of 1965 was passed, doing away with the poll tax. |
| 1968 | Brought HemisFair to San Antonio. |
| 1968 | In speech before the House, attacked Mexican American Youth Organizations and Mexican American Unity Council for propagating hateful and provoking literature and rhetoric. |
| 1969 | Chicano activist Willie Velazquez and other students heckle Henry B. at St. Mary's University. |
| 1977 | Resigned as head of House Subcommittee on Housing and Community Development. |
| 1981 | Became chairman of the House Subcommittee on Housing and Community Development. |

| 1983 | Called for the impeachment of President Reagan after the invasion of Grenada. |
| --- | --- |
| 1986 | Punched a customer at Earl Abel's restaurant for calling him a communist. |
| 1987 | Introduced legislation calling for the impeachment of President Reagan because of the Iran-Contra scandals. |
| 1988 | Forced Pentagon to calculate cost estimates resulting in the 450-bed Brooke Army Medical Center. |
| 1989 | Appointed chairman of the House Banking Finance and Urban Affairs Committee. |
| 1990 | Passed a housing bill that included his National Housing Trust. |
| 1991 | Called for the impeachment of President Bush for his actions against Iraq during the Gulf War. |
| 1994 | Republican Jim Leach took over chairmanship of Banking Committee after Republicans regained control of the House. |
| 1994 | Received the prestigious John F. Kennedy Profiles in Courage Award for his congressional crusades against corruption in the savings and loan industry and the illegal use of American-backed loans to Iraq prior to the starting of the Persian Gulf War. |
| 1997 | Fell ill with a dental infection that threatened a heart valve in July. |
| 1998 | Returned to Congress in September after being absent for fourteen months. |
| 1998 | Henry B.'s son, former judge Charlie Gonzalez, was elected to the 20th District in November. |
| 1998 | Last act as congressman was voting against |

the impeachment of President Clinton on December 19.

1998     Stepped down from his seat in Congress on December 31, after serving thirty-seven years.

1999     Watched his son Charlie be sworn in as a member of the 106th Congress on January 6, succeeding him as the representative for the 20th District.

2000     Died in San Antonio on November 28.

# CHAPTER NOTES

**Chapter 1:**

1. Interview with Bertha (Mrs. Henry B.) Gonzalez, May 18, 2001.

2. Eugene Rodriguez Jr. *Henry B. Gonzalez: A Political Profile*. Thesis: St. Mary's University, San Antonio, Texas, 1965, p. 39.

3. Carlos Guerra. "The Old 'Blowhard' Was My Hero," *San Antonio Express-News*, November 29, 2000, p. 10A.

4. Joe Holley. "Principle over Politics." *San Antonio Express-News*, Saturday, December 2, 2000, p. 8A.

5. Leslie Hicks. "A Political Burr Named Henry B." *Hispanic Business*, October 1992, p. 11. Courtesy of Henry B. Gonzalez Archives, St. Mary's University Law School.

6. Ibid., p. 14.

**Chapter 2:**

1. "Henry B. Gonzalez." *San Antonio Current*, December 3, 1992, p. 3. Reprinted with permission from *Dallas Morning News*.

2. George Carmack. "Henry B. Looks over Shoulder at His Ancesters." *San Antonio Express*, October 6, 1978, p.17A.

3. Eugene Rodriguez Jr. *Henry B. Gonzalez: A Political Profile*. Thesis: St. Mary's University, San Antonio, Texas, 1965, p. 39.

4. T. R. Fehrenbach. *Fire and Blood: A history of Mexico.*

New York: McMillan Publishing Company, Inc., 1973, p. 543.

5. Ronnie Dugger. "Conversations with a Congressman: Gonzalez of San Antonio." *The Texas Observer,* April 11, 1980, p. 8. Courtesy of Henry B. Gonzalez Archives, St. Mary's University Law School.

6. Carmack, p. 17A.

7. Dugger, p. 10.

8. Interview with Congressman Charlie Gonzalez, April 10, 2001.

9. Ibid.

10. Hart Stillwell. "Texas Rebel with a Cause." *Cornet,* August 1958, p. 43. Courtesy of Henry B. Gonzalez Archives, St. Mary's University Law School.


**Chapter 3:**

1. Interview with Congressman Charlie Gonzalez, April 10, 2001.

2. Dugger, Ronnie. "Conversations with a Congressman: Gonzalez of San Antonio," *The Texas Observer,* April 11, 1980. p. 20. Courtesy of Henry B. Gonzalez Archives, St. Mary's University Law School.

3. Ibid., p. 21.

4. Ibid.

5. Eugene Rodriguez Jr. *Henry B. Gonzalez: A Political Profile.* Thesis: St. Mary's University, San Antonio, Texas, 1965, p. 34.

6. Dugger, p. 21. Interview, Gonzalez.

7. Rodriguez, p. 39.

8. Ibid., p. 37.

9. Dugger, p. 21.

10. Ibid.

11. Rodriguez, p. 38.

12. Interview with Carlita Kosty, February 25, 2001.

13. Rodriguez, p. 39.

14. Bill Hendricks and Jaime Castillo. "Knuckle Sandwich at Eatery." *San Antonio Express-News,* November 29, 2000, p. 10A.

15. Interview with Henry B. Gonzalez Jr., June 13, 2001.

16. Ibid.

17. Rodriguez, p. 40.

18. Ibid., p. 33.

**Chapter 4:**

1. Interview with Bertha (Mrs. Henry B.) Gonzalez, May 18, 2001.

2. Ibid.

3. Ibid.

4. Ronnie Dugger. "Converstaions with a Congressman: Gonzalez of San Antonio." *The Texas Observer,* April 11, 1980, p. 22. Courtesy of Henry B. Gonzalez Archives, St. Mary's Univesity Law School.

5. Interview.

6. Eugene Rodriguez Jr. *Henry B. Gonzalez: A Political Profile.* Thesis: St. Mary's University, San Antonio, Texas, 1965, p. 41.

7. Interview.

8. Ibid.

9. Ibid.

10. Ibid.

11. Ibid.

12. Paul Thompson. "Top of the News." *San Antonio Evening News,* April 29, 1953, p. 1B.

13. Interview with Henry B. Gonzalez Jr., June 13, 2001.

14. Peyton Green. *San Antonio: City in the Sun.* New York: Whittlesey House, 1946, p. 120.

15. Rodriguez, p. 23.

16. Ibid., p. 24.

17. Ronnie Dugger. "Conversations with a Congressman: Gonzalez of San Antonio." *The Texas Observer,* May 9, 1980. p. 15. Courtesy of Henry B. Gonzalez Archives, St. Mary's University Law School.

18. Ibid.

19. Don Politico. "Legislators Unite to Meet Expected Labor Thrust." *San Antonio Light,* April 4, 1948, p. 6A.

20. Dugger, p. 15.

**Chapter 5:**
1. Ronnie Dugger. "Conversations with a Congressman: Gonzalez of San Antonio." *The Texas Observer,* May 9, 1980, p. 15. Courtesy of Henry B. Gonzalez Archives, St. Mary's University Law School.
2. Ibid.
3. Ibid., p. 16.
4. Interview with Bertha (Mrs. Henry B.) Gonzalez, May 18, 2001.
5. Dugger, p. 16.
6. Eugene Rodriguez Jr. *Henry B. Gonzalez: A Political Profile.* Thesis: St. Mary's University, San Antonio, Texas, 1965, p. 45.
7. Chris Anglim. "Remembering San Antonio's Champion of Equality—Henry B. Gonzalez (1916–2000)." *The Scholar: St. Mary's Law Review on Minority Issues,* vol. 3, no. 1, Fall 2000, p. 4. Courtesy of Chris Anglim, archivist, St. Mary's University Law School.
8. Rodriguez, p. 45.
9. Dugger, p. 16.
10. Rodriguez, p. 48.
11. Dugger, p. 16.
12. Rodriguez, p. 49.

**Chapter 6:**
1. Eugene Rodriguez Jr. *Henry B. Gonzalez: A Political Profile.* Thesis: St. Mary's University, San Antonio, Texas, 1965, p. 52.
2. Paul Burka. "Henry B. and Henry C." *The Mexican Presence,* January 1986, p. 182. Courtesy of Henry B. Gonzalez Archives, St. Mary's University Law School.
3. Ronnie Dugger. "Conversations with a Congressman: Gonzalez of San Antonio." *The Texas Observer,* May 9, 1980, p. 18. Courtesy of Henry B. Gonzalez Archives, St. Mary's University Law School.
4. Burka, p. 182.
5. Dugger, p. 15
6. Ibid.
7. Dugger, p. 18.

8. Hart Stillwell. "Texas Rebel with a Cause." *Coronet,* August 1958, p. 45. Courtesy of Henry B. Gonzalez Archives, St. Mary's University Law School.

9. Rodriguez, p. 53.

10. Interview with Maury Maverick Jr., March 27, 2001.

11. Burka, p. 220.

12. Dugger, p. 20.

13. Burka, p. 220.

14. Interview with Henry B. Gonzalez Jr., June 13, 2001.

15. Jim McCrory. "Vice President? His fans Go for It, But not HBG," *San Antonio Express-News,* January 7, 1974, p. 8-A.

16. Rodriguez, p. 63.

17. Interview with Rose Mary Gonzalez-Ramos, October 25, 2001.

18. Rodriguez, p. 64.

19. Interview with Bertha (Mrs. Henry B.) Gonzalez, May 18, 2001.

20. Dugger, p. 21.

21. Ibid., p, 22.

22. Interview, Bertha Gonzalez.

23. Rodriguez, p. 71.

24. Ibid., 72.

25. Interview, Bertha Gonzalez.

26. Dugger, p. 22.

27. Paul Thompson. "Top of the News." *San Antonio Evening News,* July 30, 1956, p. 1-B.

28. Jim McCrory. "Losing Can Be Fun, Too." *San Antonio Express-News,* July 30, 1956, p. 1-B.

29. Paul Sweeney. "Stood Up for all Americans." *San Antonio Express-News,* December 3, 2000, p. 6B.

30. James McCrory. "Post-Mortems Split on Margin." *San Antonio Light,* November 7, 1956, p. 14.

31. Dugger, p. 19.

## Chapter 7:

1. Eugene Rodriguez Jr. *Henry B. Gonzalez: A Political Profile.* Thesis: St. Mary's University, San Antonio, Texas, 1965, p. 78.

2. Ibid.

3. Joe Holley. "Principle over Politics." *San Antonio Express-News,* December 2, 2000, p. 8A.

4. Hart Stilwell. "Texas Rebel with a Cause." *Cornet,* August 1958, p. 46. Courtesy of Henry B. Gonzalez Archives, St. Mary's University Law School.

5. Ronnie Dugger. "Conversations with a Congressman: Gonzalez of San Antonio." *The Texas Observer,* May 9, 1980, p. 22. Courtesy of Henry B. Gonzalez Archives, St. Mary's University Law School.

6. Ibid.

7. Rodriguez, p. 80.

8. Dugger, p. 23.

9. Ibid.

10. Paul Burka. "Henry B. and Henry C." *The Mexican Presence,* January 1986, p. 221. Courtesy of the Henry B. Gonzalez Archives, St. Mary's University Law School.

11. "Texas: For Whom the Bell Tolls." *Time,* May 13, 1957, p. 27.

12. Ann Richards with Peter Knobler. *Straight from the Heart: My Life in Politics and Other Places.* New York: Simon and Schuster, 1989, p. 93.

13. "Daniels Choice Rejected." *San Antonio Light,* November 8, 1957, p. 14.

14. Jon Ford. "Capitol Notebook," *San Antonio Express,* October 31, 1957, p. 4-A.

15. "Daniels Finds Gonzalez Can't be Pressured." *San Antonio Light,* November 8, 1957, p. 12.

16. Rodriguez, p. 84.

17. Interview with Congressman Charlie Gonzalez, April 10, 2001.

18. Interview with Bertha (Mrs. Henry B.) Gonzalez, May 28, 2001.

19. Ibid.

20. Ibid.; Interview with Henry B. Gonzalez Jr., June 13, 2001.

21. Interview, Bertha (Mrs. Henry B.) Gonzalez.

22. Jim McCrory. "Foes Don't Dare Run Against HBG." *San Antonio Express-News,* January 6, 1974, p. 8A.

23. Fred Gantt Jr. *The Chief Executive in Texas.* Austin: The University of Texas Press, 1964, p. 278.

24. McCrory, p. 8A.

25. Rodriguez, p. 88.

26. "Gonzalez, Pena Rip Bexar Salons in River Row." *San Antonio Light,* March 4, 1959, p. 25.

27. "Gonzalez' Crystal Ball Clear." *San Antonio Light,* May 7, 1959, p. 2.

28. Jim Ford. "Gonzalez Breaking Sound Barrier." *San Antonio Express,* July 16, 1959, p. 4A.

29. Paul Thompson. "Top of the News." *San Antonio News,* July 8, 1959, p. 1B.

30. Rodriguez, p. 94.

31. "Don't Let Hoffa and Gonzalez Ruin our State." *San Antonio News,* June 1, 1960, n.p.

**Chapter 8:**

1. Interview with Maury Maverick Jr., March 27, 2001.

2. Eugene Rodriguez Jr. *Henry B. Gonzalez: A Political Profile.* Thesis: St. Mary's University, San Antonio, Texas, 1965, p. 96.

3. Ibid., p. 111.

4. Ibid., p. 112.

5. Interview with Congressman Charlie Gonzalez, April 10, 2001.

6. Ibid.

7. Ibid.

8. Ibid.

9. Paul Thompson. "Top of the News." *San Antonio News,* November 14, 1961, p. 1B.

10. Interview with Gail Beagle, June 8, 2001.

11. Carmin Danini. "Lawmaker Leaves a Grand Legacy." *San Antonio Express-News,* November 29, 2000, p. 1A.

12. Jon Ford. "Gonzalez Rules Out Ticket With Spears." *San Antonio Express,* June 7, 1959, p. 4A.

13. Rodriguez, p. 104.

14. Ibid., p. 105.

15. Interview with Henry B. Gonzalez Jr., June 13, 2001.

16. Waren Wheelock. *Henry B. Gonzalez, greater justice for all; Trini Lopez, the Latin Sound; Edward Roybal, awaken the sleeping giant.* St. Paul: EMC Corporation, 1976, p. 17.

17. Rodriguez, p. 109.

18. Wheelock, p. 18.

19. Ronnie Dugger. "Conversations with a Congressman: Gonzalez of San Antonio," *The Texas Observer,* October 17, 1980, p. 4. Courtesy of Henry B. Gonzalez Archives, St. Mary's University Law School.

## Chapter 9:

1. Paul Burka. "Henry B. and Henry C." *The Mexican Presence,* January 1986, p. 222. Courtesy of Henry B. Gonzalez Archives, St. Mary's University Law School.

2. Ibid.

3. Ibid.

4. Ronnie Dugger. "Conversations with a Congressman: Gonzalez of San Antonio." *The Texas Observer,* December 12, 1980, p. 11. Courtesy Henry B. Gonzalez Archives, St. Mary's University Law School.

5. Ibid.

6. Ibid.

7. Ibid.

8. Burka, p. 223.

9. Dugger, p. 16.

10. Burka, p. 223.

11. Ronnie Dugger. "Conversations with a Congressman: Gonzalez of San Antonio." *The Texas Observer,* October 17, 1980, p. 4. Courtesy Henry B. Gonzalez Archives, St. Mary's University Law School.

12. Leslie Hicks. "A Political Burr Named Henry B." *Hispanic Business,* October 1992, p. 10. Courtesy Henry B. Gonzalez Archives, St. Mary's University Law School.

13. Hubert H. Humphrey. *The Education of a Public Man:*

*My Life and Politics.* Garden City, New York: Doubleday & Company, Inc., 1976, p. 143.

14. Ronnie Dugger. *The Politician: The Life and Times of Lyndon Johnson.* New York: W.W. Norton & Company, 1982, p. 143.

15. Eugene Rodriguez Jr. *Henry B. Gonzalez: A Political Profile.* Thesis: St. Mary's University, San Antonio, Texas, 1965, p. 148.

16. Paul Starobin. "Double Trouble." *National Journal,* January 12, 1991, p. 61.

17. James McCrory. "Gonzalez Never Forgets—Just Ask One Foe." *San Antonio News,* January 8, 1974, p. 9A.

18. Ibid.

19. Ibid.

20. Loyd Larrabee. "Democratic Fued Takes a Breather as JFK Visits." *San Antonio Express,* November 22, 1963, p. 1A.

21. Ann Richards with Peter Knobler. *Straight from the Heart: My life in Politics and Other Places.* New York: Simon & Schuster, 1989, p. 119.

22. James McCrory. "Gonzalez Sees Mrs. Kennedy Kiss President Last Goodbye." *San Antonio Express-News,* November 23, 1963, p. 16A.

23. Ibid.

## Chapter 10:

1. Lady Bird Johnson. *A White House Diary.* New York: Holt Rinehart and Winston, 1970, p. 464.

2. Rick Casey. "The Best HBG Story I've Heard." *San Antonio Express-News,* December 13, 2000, p. 3A.

3. Leslie Hicks. "A Political Burr Named Henry B." *Hispanic Business,* October 1992, p. 14. Courtesy of Henry B. Gonzalez Archives, St. Mary's University Law School.

4. Interview with Mary Jesse (Susie) Roque, April 10, 2001.

5. Ibid.

6. Ibid.

7. Delores Gamez. "Letter to Editor." *San Antonio Express-*

*News,* December 12, 2000, p. 4B.

8. Interview with Bertha (Mrs. Henry B.) Gonzalez, May 18, 2001.

9. Ibid.

10. Interview with Congressman Charlie Gonzalez, April 10, 2001.

11. Interview with Henry B. Gonzalez Jr., June 13, 2002.

12. Ibid.

13. E-mail: Tod Wells, May 15, 2001.

14. Interview, April 11, 2001.

15. Interview, June 13, 2001.

16. Ibid.

17. Interview with Carlita Kosty, February 25, 2001.

18. Ibid.

19. Eiginio Rodriguez. "Letter to Editor." *San Antonio Express-News,* December 2, 2000, p. 6B.

20. Interview with Lucille Santos, April 13, 2001.

21. E-mail: Tod Wells.

22. Jim McCrory. "Gonzalez Never Forgets—Just Ask One Foe." *San Antonio News,* January 8, 1974, p. 9A.

23. Interview with Gail Beagle, June 8, 2001.

24. Ibid.

25. Ibid.

26. Interview, April 10, 2001.

**Chapter 11:**

1. Ronnie Dugger. Conversations with a Congressman: Gonzalez of San Antonio." *The Texas Observer,* March 28, 1980, p. 6. Courtesy Henry B. Gonzalez Archives, St. Mary's University Law School.

2. Ibid.

3. Leslie Hicks. "A Political Burr Named Henry B." *Hispanic Business,* October 1992, p. 18. Courtesy Henry B. Gonzalez Archives: St. Mary's University Law School.

4. Dugger, p. 6.

5. Ibid., p. 8.

6. Ibid.

7. Ibid., p. 12.

8. Ibid.

9. Ibid.

10 Ibid., p. 9.

11. Sherry Sylvester. "Henry B. Was Right." *San Antonio Express-News,* December 11, 2000, p. 6A.

12. Bill Hendricks and Jaime Castillo. "Knuckle Sandwich at Eatery." *San Antonio Express-News,* November 29, 2000, p. 10A.

13. Interview with Henry B. Gonzalez Jr., June 13, 2001.

14. Judith Graham et.al. *February 1993 Current Biography,* vol. 54 no. 2, New York: The H. W. Wilson Company, 1993, p. 28. Courtesy Henry B. Gonzalez Archives, St. Mary's University Law School).

15. Judith Graham et. al. *Current Biography Yearbook 1993.* New York: The H. W. Wilson Company, 1993, p. 217.

16. "Banking Chairman a Contrast in Styles." *San Antonio Express-News,* January 4, 1989, p. 10B.

17. Leslie Hicks. "HBG's Classic Quest: Gonzalez Compared to Dante." *San Antonio Express-News,* June 10, 1990, p. 1D.

18. Ibid., 6D.

19. Ibid.

20. Ibid.

21. Ibid.

22. Bruce Davidson. "Politician of the Year: Henry B. Gonzalez Rattles Capitol Hill." *San Antonio Express-News,* December 31, 1989, p. 5N.

23. Gary Martin. "A Legend and a Lightning Rod." *San Antonio Express-News,* December 2, 2000, p. 7B.

24. Paul Sweeny. "Letter to Editor." *San Antonio Express-News,* December 2, 2000, p. 6B.

**Chapter 12:**

1. Jamie Castillo. "HBG Returns to Office, Work at Capitol Hill." *San Antonio Express-News,* September 24, 1998, p. 1A.

2. Ibid., p. 10A.

3. Jamie Castillo. "HBG Takes a Bow on the House

Floor." *San Antonio Express-News,* September 25, 1998, p. 1A.

    4. Gary Martin. "Gonzalez Takes Clinton's Side." *San Antonio Express-News,* August 23, 1998, p. 1A.

    5. Ibid.

    6. Ibid., p. 1A.

    7. Editorial, "Henry B., People's Choice for 45 Years, Is One in a Million." *San Antonio Express-News,* November 28, 1998, p. 2G.

    8. Castillo, September 24, 1998, p. 10A.

    9. Jim Wright. "'Legend' a Fitting Description of Henry B. Gonzalez." *Fort Worth Star Telegram,* November 30, 1977, p. 3D. Courtesy Henry B. Gonzalez Archives, St. Mary's University Law School.

    10. James McCrory. "What Makes Henry B. Run?" *San Antonio Express-News,* January 6, 1974, p. 1H.

    11. Interview with Carlita Kosty, February 25, 2001.

    12. Wright, p. 3D.

    13. Paul Burka. "Henry B. and Henry C." *The Mexican Presence,* January 1986, p. 223. Courtesy Henry B. Gonzalez Archives, St. Mary's University Law School.

    14. Rick Casey. "HBG a Fighter for Better or Worse." *San Antonio Express-News,* November 29, 2000, p. 3A.

    15. Robert Moreno. "Henry B. Gonzalez." *Unidos,* May/June, 1991, p. 16. Courtesy Henry B. Gonzalez Archives, St. Mary's University Law School.

    16. Leslie Hicks. "HBG's Classic Quest: Gonzalez Compared to Dante," *San Antonio Express-News,* June 10, 1990, p. 6D.

    17. Winton Pitcoff. "Congressman Henry Gonzalez." *Shelter Force,* March/April 1998, p. 21. Courtesy Henry B. Gonzalez Archives, St. Mary's University Law School.

    18. Veronica Salazar. "Dedication Rewarded: Prominent Mexican-Americans." *San Antonio Express,* April 22, 1973, p. 13.

    19. McCrory, p. 8A.

    20. Maury Maverick. "Henry B.'s Values, Spirit Still at Work for Public." *San Antonio Express-News,* July 19, 1998, p. 3G.

21. Interview with Congressman Charlie Gonzalez, April 10, 2001.

22. Martin, p. 28A.

23. Carmina Danini. "Crowd Chants 'Viva Henry B.' One Last Time." *San Antonio Express-News,* December 2, 2000, p. 1A.

24. Ibid. p. 8A.

25. Carlos Guerra. "Celebrate HBG, Mourn the Real Loss." *San Antonio Express-News,* November 30, 2000, p. 1B.

26. Maverick, p. 3G.

27. Cary Clack. "A Thank You From One You Served." *San Antonio Express-News,* December 2, 2000, p. 1B.

# GLOSSARY

**amateur:** one who engages in study, science, or sport as a pastime.

**animosity:** ill will or resentment; hostility.

**catalyst:** an agent that provokes or causes change or action.

**commission:** a group of persons directed to perform some duty.

**communist:** one who does not believe in owning private property.

**conservative:** marked by moderation or caution.

**executioner:** one who puts another person to death.

**filibuster:** to talk nonstop in an attempt to delay or prevent action.

**immigrant:** a person who comes to a country to live permanently.

**inauguration:** to induct into an office.

**liberal:** generous, bountiful, giving freely, open-minded.

**maverick:** an independent individual who does not go along with a group or party.

**orator:** a public speaker.

**philosophy:** an analysis of fundamental beliefs.

**passionate:** expressing intense feelings.

**populist:** a believer in the rights, wisdom, or virtues of the common people.

**potential:** something that can develop.

**revolutionist:** on bringing about major change.

**tuberculosis:** a highly contagious disease that primarily affects the lungs.

# FURTHER READING

Bandon, Alexandra. *Mexican Americans.* Columbus, Ohio: Silver Burdett Press, 1993.

Bode, Janet. *The Colors of Freedom: Immigrant Stories.* Danbury, Connecticut: Franklin Watts, 1999.

Brimner, Larry D. *A Migrant Family.* Minneapolis, Minnesota: The Lerner Publishing Group, 1992.

Bennett, Michele and Barbara. *Twenty-Two Texas Women: Strong, Tough, and Independent.* Austin, Texas: Eakin Press, 1996.

Catalano, Julie. *The Mexican Americans.* Broomall, Pennsylvania: Chelsea House Publishers, 1995.

Crawford, Ann Fears, and Crystal Sasse Ragsdale. *Women in Texas: Their Lives; Their Experiences; Their Accomplishments.* Burnet, Texas: Eakin Press, 1982.

Davis, Lucile, et al. *Cesar Chavez.* Mankato, Minnesota: Capstone Press, Inc., 1997.

Flynn, Jean. *Texas Women Who Dared to Be First.* Austin, Texas, Eakin Press, 1999.

Hadden, Gerald. *Teenage Refugees from Mexico Speak Out.* New York: The Rosen Publishing Group, Inc., 1997.

Kramer, Jon. *Lee Trevino.* Orlando, Florida: Raintree Steck-Vaughn Publishers, 1996.

Lasher, Patricia. *Texas Women: Interviews and Images.* Photographs by Beverley Bentley. Austin, Texas: Republic of Texas Press, 1996.

Mavis, Barbara. *Rafael Palmeiro.* Bear, Delaware: Mitchell Lane Publishers, Inc., 1997.

McKissack, Patricia, et al. *Booker T. Washington: Leader & Educator.* Berkeley Heights, New Jersey: Enslow Publishers, Inc., 1992.

———. *Paul Robeson: A Voice to Remember.* Berkeley Heights, New Jersey: Enslow Publishers, Inc., 1992.

Perez, Frank. *Dolores Huerta.* Orlando, Florida: Raintree Steck-Vaughn Publishers, 1995.

Romero, Maritza. *Selena Perez: Queen of Tejano Music.* New York: The Rosen Publishing Group, Inc., 1997.

Stefoff, Rebecca. *Gloria Estefan.* Boomall, Pennsylvania: Chelsea House Publishers, 1995.

# SUGGESTED ACTIVITIES

The following suggestions can be adapted to different grade levels.

1. a. **Students:** Find as many outstanding minorities as you can in your history textbook. Write one sentence about each person and include dates if possible.

   b. **Teacher:** Lead students in a discussion of their research, emphasizing changes over the years, particularly after the Civil Rights Act of 1965.

2. a. **Students:** Talk to a family member, friend, or neighbor and write one paragraph about prejudice that he or she has experienced.

   b. **Teacher:** Allow students to read paragraphs aloud and discuss what they can do to avoid prejudice or to change attitudes.

3. a. **Students:** List all representatives in your school's voting district. Identify the representatives as Democrat or Republican: Texas House of Representatives, Texas Senate, U.S. House of Representatives, U.S. Senate.

b. **Teacher:** Discuss assignment in class and emphasize the importance of the representatives' stand on issues regardless of ethnicity.

4. a. **Students:** Read a book, fiction or nonfiction, that deals with prejudice. As you read, make a note of the pages that deal with prejudice.

   b. **Teachers:** Have students write a short report describing the prejudices they found and how they feel about it. If time allows, let students read their reports in class and discuss them.

# INDEX

139